THE
SECRET
PREMIER
LEAGUE
DIARY OF A
CARDIFF
CITY FAN

DAVID COLLINS &
GARETH BENNETT

Dedicated to you.
All of you.

'Hope is the only thing stronger than fear.'

Suzanne Collins, *The Hunger Games*

First published 2014

The History Press
The Mill, Brimscombe Port
Stroud, Gloucestershire, GL5 2QG
www.thehistorypress.co.uk

British Library Cataloguing in Publication Data.
A catalogue record for this book is available from the
British Library.

ISBN 978 0 7509 5958 2

Typesetting and origination by The History Press
Printed in Great Britain

CONTENTS

FOREWORD

I was so pleased to be asked to support this book.

For this book is like no other book you will read. It is written through the eyes of a football supporter, for a football supporter. It is packed with opinion, news and comment about a momentous year in the history of Cardiff City Football Club. The highs and lows, the goals and near misses, the pies and the pints! The boys have told their story as they see it. Some will agree with their interpretation of events, some will disagree, but all will enjoy.

David and Gareth have captured the emotion, hopes, and sometimes the frustrations, of all Cardiff City fans in a unique and appealing format. For me, they have conveyed the true passion of those who follow this famous club, and I know all about that, believe me!

The diary is an excellent way to map the journey of the Bluebirds in the Premier League and fans, I am sure, will relate to it.

I am just hoping for a happy ending!!

Jason Perry
2013
344 first team appearances for Cardiff City
1987–1997

INTRODUCTION

It's 2013.

Cardiff City had swept all before them.

We can talk about red, we can talk about blue, but what cannot be denied is that Cardiff City fans everywhere could enjoy an early night every Saturday, as Manish gives way to Gary, and enjoy a curry and Cardiff City on *Match of the Day*.

Alan Hansen will tell Caulker to get tighter and Shearer will explain how Fraizer Campbell could have got away from David Luiz. Or will they? The point is, we simply don't know.

As the subtitle suggests, this is a real diary. And if you have kept a diary, you know the surprises fate may have in store. You might buy that fancy shirt on a Friday, but you don't know if you will pull on a Saturday until the diary reveals its secrets on Sunday morning. She could stand you up on Tuesday, meet your mother on Wednesday or bring her straighteners and slippers over by Thursday. It's a hairy existence.

Like any diary, it's written in real time, day by day. We know not how it will end. Adrian Mole could marry Pandora, Samuel Pepys could invent the fire extinguisher or Declan John could join Real Madrid. We simply have no idea. Basically, we have written a book without knowing how the story ends. Robinson Crusoe would never have gone for it. But we know that you will trust every word, because, like us, you live, breathe, and probably die, by Cardiff City.

When the film of this book is made, it will probably be a disaster movie. We hope that it will be *Harry Potter and the*

4th Place Finish, yet we all know that it will be *Carry on up the Creek without a Paddle*.

Welcome to Cardiff City. Day by day.

Gareth Bennett & David Collins
2013

MEET THE
DIARISTS

To be honest, you're probably sick to death of us already.

We are both veterans of Cardiff City matches over many, many years. You will have read the fanzines which Gareth produced back in the '90s ('O Bluebird of Happiness'), or reminisced with David as he unfolded his collection of match programmes in those publications.

In later years, you may have cursed us both, as we tested your knowledge of all things Cardiff City through the Never Mind the Bluebirds series of quiz books – oft imitated, never bettered, by the way.

Gareth is the more studious of the two, maybe. He is also prone to moments of cynicism, as you will discover. David is a full-on Facebook keyboard warrior, wandering the message boards under the pseudonym 'Pontprennau Bluebird'. Gareth has no time for such nonsense.

David hosts the popular Cardiff City Phone-in on GTFM and Bro Radio. He is a passionate Welsh speaker. Gareth can just about pronounce Llanrumney, and holds no interest in events in 'Presthisin' or 'Presthatyn'.

We mused at length over how to set the book out. Should we write a day each? Or a month each? Do we simply pretend that we are one big person and write everything as 'we', imagining that we both attended every game, event and pub-crawl described in these pages? Nah, that wouldn't work. That would merely look contrived, we decided.

Eventually, we agreed that we would simply each write our own entries as the season unfolds, and cut-and-paste them as we go along. You will see that Gareth tends to write the match reports, and David covers the midweek gossip. Both of us wander off the point constantly. We have used different fonts to help you see whose bit is whose. David's bits are like this ... *Gareth's bits are like this.* You'll get the hang of it.

No doubt you will recognise your own lives through these pages – the ups, the downs, the hopes and glory. Relive our hangovers, share our disappointments. Years from now you will find this diary hidden in the attic amongst the Christmas decorations. What's the betting you leave it up there too?

One

OH WHAT A NIGHT

Dear Diary,

Wednesday, 17 April 2013

Wow, what a night.

All home safe now, but it's been a messy one. Jeans are in a heap on the floor. One lonely shoe on the stairs. Random coins lay scattered across the bedside table. The remains of a large kebab occupy the kitchen table. Surely if God had wanted to us to drink, then why create hangovers? Coffee. Where is the ruddy coffee ...?

Last night was a blur. We met in the Corporation, I remember that much. But then, we always meet there, so that may not be a strong start. No definitely – it was definitely the Corporation. Definitely.

Or perhaps Wetherspoons ...

Many Cardiff City games are a blur, of course. Last night though, remains especially hazy. It was at home. It was Charlton Athletic, I think. Charlton play in red though, and we play in ....

Oh, let's not go there this morning. I don't remember any goals, though. So why did we celebrate so hard? Surely we didn't lose? Would my head hurt so much even after a 0-0 draw? Surely not ...

Dear Diary,

Sunday, 5 May 2013

Ah this is better ... a blazing hot, sunny day, a victory parade and only £10 for our 'We are Premier League' t-shirts. Bliss. A beautiful day.

A chance now to relax and enjoy the summer holidays. Break out the sun tan oil boys ...

Dear Diary,

Sunday, 11 August 2013

WTF ...???!!

Malky has gone ballistic in the transfer market. Cornelius looks a decent buy, and Caulker from Spurs is a bit of a coup; but Gary Medel? Off of Sevilla?? He is, like, a proper player! Yogi watches La Liga on his iPhone and ruddy raves about him. He is all over YouTube, this fella – bicycle kicks, World Cup appearances, seven red cards.

The story goes that he even kept Lionel Messi quiet when playing against Barca at the Nou Camp. That's as maybe – but could he shackle Andy Carroll in the East End??

Friday, 16 August 2013

So, are we all set then?

Dear Diary,

Saturday, 17 August 2013

The Day has Dawned ... fifty years of hurt would be over today. The Longest Day.

I have negotiated a 7.00 a.m. slot on Radio Wales, reviewing the papers. The *Western Mail* story about New York being gripped by 'Sacker' fervour is the obvious lead. Apparently, the various districts of New York have been assigned a different Premier League team to follow – and Brooklyn has been allocated Cardiff City! I tell the listeners, 'I won't be happy until Barack Obama is seen doing the Ayatollah, but it's a start.'

West Ham United 2 – 0 Cardiff City

k/o 3.00 p.m.

Thanks to rigorous close season planning, we elect not to travel to our first away game at West Ham United. This is going to be a season where away trips have to be planned, and budgeted for. Having both enjoyed the warmth of an East End welcome in the 2012 play-off semi-final, we elect for the slightly gentler environs of the Queens Vaults, Westgate Street, for this moment in history. We await our first game in the Premier League. The West Ham academy. Bobby Moore, Trevor Brooking and Alf Garnett. It doesn't get tougher than this.

Actually, on paper, the fixture does not seem too bad. We recall a fortuitous victory at Upton Park on the first weekend of the Championship two years ago, thanks to King Kenny. Andy Carroll is also out injured, so perhaps we will be in with a shout.

Various pubs in Cardiff are known to be showing the City's Premier League games live. The Queen's Vaults in the city centre has been advertising this for some time. We arrive to find the pub rammed with bodies, and fight to the bar. There is much interest in the early kick-off, Liverpool v. Stoke, which is occupying people's attention while (so we presume) they are waiting for the City game to begin.

By the time we have the first pints in, the Liverpool game has finished. To our amazement, people begin streaming out of the pub, leaving a gap at the front, where we duly stand. We look around and assess the diminished numbers in the pub. Although it is still busy, it is not as packed as it was ten minutes ago. (Amazing how many Liverpudlians have settled in Cardiff over the years, eh? Most of these 'Reds' have never been to Liverpool, and would struggle to locate it on a map of Britain. Sad that these armchair and bar-room clowns have no interest whatever in their home town team being in the Premier League.)

Fellow sufferers Sam and Andy arrive. (I always call them Sam and Ella. They never get the joke.) Andy is optimistic about our chances. He has looked at a league table in the paper and we were already third, below Arsenal and Aston Villa! I told him he should cut it out and pin it on his kitchen wall.

It's a 3.00 p.m. kick-off. History is over. Real life starts here. Albanian TV has secured clear vision and decent sound quality. More beer arrives. Could get used to watching away games here.

After 12 minutes, West Ham's left-winger, Matt Jarvis, burns down the wing and pulls the ball back. It falls on the edge of the box, where Joe Cole takes it with his back to goal. No problem here then, we think – only for Cole to turn on a sixpence and, in the same movement, swing his right foot at the ball, which ends up buried in the far corner of the net.

More scares follow, and City struggle to actually get into the attacking half of the pitch. However, we spot a break-out chance, when our Korean wonder-boy, Kim, dashes clear, counter-attacking from a West Ham corner. There is not much support, and Kim ends up firing a shot wide. Bellamy gives him some 'verbals' for not waiting for him to catch up, but to be honest, Bellers was some distance behind Kim, and the Korean may not have even seen or heard him. The fact that Bellers is not able to get up there is worrying …

The 10 minutes before half-time are much better. City retain possession for long periods, and seem to be getting on top. The fact that we do not create anything worth mentioning with all this possession is neither here nor there!

The second half begins in much the same way, with City having more of the ball. We wondered before the season whether Fraizer Campbell (and the other strikers) would be up to the mark – would their finishing be sharp enough for the Premier League? Here, though, what was worse was that not a single chance was created during this period when we were on top. When we had an occasional free-kick in a danger area – which was where a lot of our goals came from last season – Whittingham did little with it. In fact, Whitts looked tense and drawn throughout. He has always been a nervous character, hasn't he? Often lacking confidence, and he looked today as if he would rather be enjoying his football back in the Championship. This Premier League malarkey looked like it was all a bit too much for him.

We knew that City would eventually be punished for their ineffectualness by another West Ham goal. It came 15 minutes from the end, when Cole passed inside from the right to Kevin Nolan, who was standing minding his own business on the edge of our penalty area. There were plenty of City defenders about, but it didn't occur to any of them to actually go and mark him. Hmm, perhaps they will learn ... Before we had a chance to blink, the ball was in the back of our net and Nolan was running towards the home fans doing the 'clucking chicken' celebration that he started at Newcastle.

And that was that. Malky at least tried to change things and, having had only one striker for most of the game, we then ended it with three, with big Rudy Gestede and quick Nicky Maynard joining Campbell up front. This produced one chance (finally!) when Connolly, our right-back, who supposedly has a nosebleed if he gets over the halfway line, actually went almost to the byline and crossed the ball low into the box. It seemed to be heading straight for Maynard, who was arriving about 3 yards from goal but, just as the ball reached him, a West Ham defender managed to get his foot in and the ball somehow bobbled over the bar. Right in front of 3,000 City fans. More beer arrives ...

Later, we review the anguish thanks to YouTube. Repeated viewings show Cole's opener as a bit of a wonder-goal. Could we have defended better? True, Jarvis beat Connolly down the line, and if we had a quicker full-back, maybe he would have blocked the cross. But Jarvis is quick over 5 yards, and may beat most Premier League full-backs once in a game.

And that was all he did really – beat him once. The cross was pulled back so deep that it didn't seem that dangerous – but Cole managed to bring off a shot on the turn. Caulker had tracked to the byline to block the cross at the near-post, so he wasn't at fault. Medel, our new Chilean midfield tackler, was closest to Cole, but not close enough to block the shot. Would any defender have got close enough to him, quickly enough, to have blocked it? Somehow I doubt it.

Amazingly, Cole has only scored 12 Premier League goals for West Ham before now. This one was, for us, the unlucky 13th. If he has only scored 13 for them (in 138 appearances), does that mean most defenders can deal with him – but we couldn't? Or does it mean that when he does score, they tend to be wonder-goals which nobody can defend against? Hopefully the latter!

The second goal was far worse. Caulker was standing 3ft away from Nolan for what seemed like 10 minutes before the ball arrived. He didn't seem to think he was under any obligation to move any closer. The replay shows Caulker standing to one side of him, and then, as Cole gets the ball, instead of realising the danger, Caulker moves closer to the other centre-back, Turner, leaving Nolan even more space than he had before. Connolly is standing a couple of yards the other side of Nolan, also marking nobody, but he doesn't realise what Caulker is going to do, and doesn't have enough time to react to the situation. So all Nolan has done is stand on the edge of the box and wait for someone to come and mark him, but no one does. And Caulker is our £7 million defender?! Last season's captain, Mark Hudson, who Caulker is keeping out of the side, would have just closed down Nolan and blocked the shot.

As for this 'one up front' business – it occurs that if we start with one, and then end with three up there, then a suitable compromise might be: play the whole bloody game with two … Ah well, what do we know …?

We switch our post-match attentions to checking out the results of our fellow PL sides. Limited interest in Bournemouth v. Wigan. Villa win easily at the Emirates. Lambert scores again for Southampton – that's quite a week he has had.

By 6.00 p.m., it was back on Radio Wales for the Rob Phillips Football Phone-in (helpfully called 'Phone Rob Phillips').

Nathan Blake and David Giles strongly rebut my claim that the substitutions cost us the result, presenting cogent arguments about needing to make something happen in the game. Ah, what do they know? Let's get back to the telly.

Swansea have crashed to Man. U. in the tea-time kick-off and the league table shows them below us on goal average. Cries of 'You're going down with the Gooners!' fill the pub. Things are looking up.

Dear Diary,
Sunday, 18 August 2013

Our long-awaited debut on *Match of the Day* saw us take the last place in the show. Our defensive horror show is spared Hansen's glare. Thank heavens for small mercies.

Chelsea's Sunday afternoon victory over Hull amazingly pushes City up a place on alphabetical order. Arsenal move up a spot, but the Jacks stay rock bottom. If Man. City stuff Newcastle by 3 or more tomorrow we could be out of the relegation places!! These kick-off times are going to take some getting used to.

Dear Diary,
Monday, 19 August 2013

Manchester City 4 Newcastle 0!! This Premier League's a ruddy doddle! (Hope the Jacks enjoy being stuck in a relegation dogfight all season ...)

Dear Diary,
Wednesday, 21 August 2013

On a quiet day for news we resort to checking out some facts about our next opponents. We get as far as Manchester City's speed merchant Jesus Navas. Turns out this lad can run at a speed of 33.35kph (or 20.72mph). Blimey, he'd have to slow down outside schools if that is true.

Dear Diary,

Sunday, 25 August 2013

Sunday. The fourteenth Sunday after Pentecost. Our first real Sunday in the Premier League. This is the Day Vincent Tan has Made, Let us Rejoice and be Glad in it, and be Glad in it.

The intricacies of the Sky TV staggered kick-off-times' schedule have returned us, for now, to the bottom three. No matter. For it's a full and expectant house at the Cardiff City Stadium, as the media spotlight turns its full glare on CF11. Standing room only in every pub in the city.

Cardiff City 3 – 2 Manchester City

k/o 4.00 p.m.

OK, we won't go on too much about this one. Everyone was either there, or saw it, or heard about it. Initially, my reaction is one of exultation. But I am a natural pessimist, so when I got up the following day and started thinking about this … This was a classic smash-and-grab raid. Like a Cup tie. They had all the possession, couldn't do anything with it. We went up the field and scored 3 goals, 2 of them from corners, and won. But how many times is that going to happen? How many games are we going to win with minimal possession? Ah, but we are not going to play Man. City every week. No, that is true. But everyone is going to know we score goals from corners now, and they are going to defend them properly.

Let's look at this objectively. Marshall is fine, couldn't do anything about the goals. Caulker and Turner defended well, with Medel and Gunnarsson in front of them forming a solid wall. Oh, Medel is the guy from Spain, only he is actually from Chile. They call him 'El Pit Bull', although that is odd, do they call those dogs 'pit bulls' in Spain? That sounds a bit implausible – anyway, I digress.

On the flanks, Bellers and Whitts came back and 'doubled up' well. That means they retreated and helped out the full-backs. Going forward, they did nothing. So now we are picking wide men for their ability to come back and defend – but we won't be playing Man. City every week, you've gotta keep telling yourself that.

Kim looked dangerous. Gunnarsson pushed forward into the box and finished well for his goal. Campbell did really well to get into 'the right areas' and grab his goals. This is going to look good on Sky (AND some of it actually does!). Gary Neville is impressed with the atmosphere at the stadium – and for the first time, after four years, the stadium did actually sound as noisy as Ninian Park. The newspaper writers are talking of 'passion' and 'fervour'. We could have some fun here with the home games this season.

But … but … When you see it again, we are ceding lots of possession to Man. City. This really was a smash-and-grab raid. We showed plenty of pluck and spirit, and the fervour of the crowd certainly helped – but we were a bit lucky. We will not be that lucky – or even that plucky – every week. But then, the fervour of the crowd will surely help us to win other games, too.

Back at the pub Sam tells me that we are 'trending on Twitter'. I don't know what this means at all, but apparently it's quite good.

Dear Diary,

Monday, 26 August 2013

Manic Monday.

We learned a new expression today, 'going viral'.

If ever a day was created to herald a new dawn, this was it.

Early morning traffic was virtually non-existent as South Wales took advantage of the bank holiday to sleep off its collective hangover. Eventually, bodies stumbled into motion to discover that, elsewhere, the world had finally discovered Cardiff City. Message boards had been in meltdown, Google scored record searches on Cardiff City and even the Twittersphere was on it. Radio phone-ins all over South Wales lapped it all up and fed it back to a gleeful audience. A pleasure which does not cloy.

Those of us who also enjoy more traditional means of keeping up with the modern world, gleefully snapped up all the newspaper copy available. The local boys went ape-shit of course, but even the Fleet Street red tops and broadsheets could not hide their glee at the biggest story so far this season.

People with no previous Cardiff City connections jumped on the bandwagon of course (who is Sam Warburton??) as the names of Vincent Tan and Fraizer Campbell adorned sports pages from New York, across to Malaysia and even the *Sydney Herald* – they were all full of Cardiff City. For years we had sung about the 'Greatest team in football the world has ever seen' ... and now they're gonna believe us.

Dear Diary,

Wednesday, 28 August 2013

Accrington Stanley 0 – 2 Cardiff City

k/o 7.45 p.m.

ALL RIGHT, I know this book is supposed to be a Premier League diary – and Accrington Stanley are very much NOT in the Premier League. But we still get to play them – three days after we have beaten Manchester City. What a sequence of games! That is the beauty of the fixture list.

I started going regularly to City games about twenty-five years ago, and for the first fifteen years we were always in the two lower divisions. We didn't even get to the Championship until a decade ago, so Accrington Stanley is the sort of team we used to play in those days. Although we didn't actually play Stanley, because they weren't in the league at the time. In fact, we have never played Stanley before, home or away. All the more reason to make this my first away trip of the season!

What you do is, you get a Megabus to Manchester. This costs you £5. The only trouble is, it leaves Cardiff city centre at 5.30 in the morning, so you have to be up pretty early to get it. Also, as you have bought your seat reservation online, you don't actu-ally have a physical ticket to show the driver. So if you are still unsure of this new-fangled high technology world in which we live, it's a bit scary when you approach the driver and all you have is a reservation number which you have scribbled down on a random old envelope yourself. I mean, this number could be anything – I could have made it up off the top of my head while I was sitting on the toilet that morning, and written it down.

But amazingly, it satisfies the driver, I am allowed to board the coach, and this moment of techno-induced paranoia passes.

The coach takes you to Manchester, and you try to remember the way from this 'Shudehill Interchange' place – which is the coach station – to the railway station. You think you remember the way, and then you see a sign with directions to 'Manchester Piccadilly' and 'Manchester Victoria', and then you realise, or remember, that there are actually two central railway stations in Manchester. And you realise that you forgot to write down which one gets you to Accrington. Well, Piccadilly is the station you get to if you are coming from Cardiff. Cardiff is south of Manchester. So that station is presumably dealing with points south. Accrington is north of Manchester. So that must be the other station ... Then, having decided all this (on the basis of some fairly large assumptions), you find the signs run out and you cannot actually find 'Manchester Victoria'. Does it exist? You ask someone, and they say, jokily, 'It's just there', pointing to a bit of scaffolding, and some protective hoardings. And then it turns out that, behind the hoarding, there is a major railway interchange cunningly hidden away.

So can I get from here to Accrington, I ask at the ticket office. Yes, but only via Blackburn, I am told. (Would there have been any other way?) Okay, so I have to find a train going to Blackburn. I look at the big TV console with the details of all the outgoing trains, which isn't very good, because it keeps flashing new information up every few seconds. And none of the trains seem to terminate at Blackburn. There are so many trains coming up and then flashing away again, to be replaced by details of other trains, that it is impossible (unless you have been trained to be an RAF fighter pilot) to make any sense of it. Certainly there is not enough time to see if 'Blackburn' is flashing up as one of the stops on any of these trains.

Eventually, after a process of trial and error, involving going to different platforms to see where the trains are going (and stopping), I manage to get the Clitheroe train, which is the one actually stopping at Blackburn. Yeah, Clitheroe – I should have known that, shouldn't I! Maybe they could have told me that at the ticket office. So I get on the right train, and look out of the window. We soon get out of Manchester, and it gets quite rural. After a bit, there are rolling hills and fields, and all the houses are built of whitish stone. It's getting a bit 'Last of the Summer Wine'. Then we get to Blackburn, there's only four platforms, so it's easy to work out where to stand to get the connection to 'Accy', and the next thing I know, I am there. In Accy. Phew.

The place is a reasonably sized market town, with a bit of bustle about it. There are at least half a dozen pubs doing a decent trade on this midweek afternoon. The football ground is a mile or two out of the town centre, and initially you can't actually see it from the main road, because it is so tucked away. Then you go down a flight of steps, and suddenly a small stand is before you.

The City fans are on the away end, an old-fashioned open terrace behind one of the goals. The stands are all very shallow, and the two on the side of the pitch only go back about ten or twelve rows! I have only been to two league grounds less impressive than this. Maidstone United (who played at Dartford) was similarly small but even pokier – at least here, you can see the surrounding fields. Scarborough was less developed, because the two ends behind the goals had no stands, no nothing – just a view of a council estate in the distance. So the 'Store First Stadium' (formerly known as the Crown Ground) is better than both of those. I would say only the third worst league ground I have ever been to.

There is amusement to be had in such a place, though.

There is a game taking place on an adjoining parks football pitch, and the participating players are amused to find themselves the subjects of various chants directed from the away end. For a while, it seems as though this game is more the focus of attention than the Capital One Cup tie which is taking place in front of us. Actually, this parks game is a bit more interesting!

Okay, you can only watch a parks game for so long. The joke is wearing thin; those parks players must be starting to think we are proper loonies or something.

So on to the 'real' game: City are fielding their second team. Before the game, in the stadium shop – I hesitate to call it a 'stadium shop', because is this ground really a 'stadium'? But anyway … – a City supporter was explaining to the Accy guy selling him a programme that City won't actually be fielding any of the team that beat Man. City. 'Really?' the guy asks, looking confused. 'What, none of them?' The City guy shakes his head.

'No, it's the Second team out tonight.' Accy takes the money and gives him the programme, looking dazed. Of course, Accy don't really have a Second team. They can barely muster a First team. This is what it's like down at this level of the league. I am beginning to remember it again from City's past. Okay, so City are fielding a Second team. This gives me a chance to have a look at this Second team.

Years ago, you could do this by going to see a 'reserve game'. Now they don't call them 'reserve games'. They call them 'Capital One Cup games'. In January and February, they call them 'FA Cup games'. Right, so how is City's Second team shaping up? Not very well, I fear. The full-backs are going forward quite well (John Brayford, who we have just signed from Derby, and a young kid called Declan John); but the centre-backs, Mark Hudson and Kevin McNaughton, are not very good at advancing with the ball. We have two guys in central midfield – Don Cowie and the strangely named Jordon Mutch – who both think they are playing 'up the field', and neither of them are bothering to try to come back and 'build through the midfield'.

Eventually, after about half an hour of watching Hudson's booted balls floating up into the night sky, they decide to 'take it in turns' to come deep and accept some passes. Then City start stringing some possession together. We have two wingers with something to prove, Tommy Smith on the right, and Craig Noone on the left. They don't really play like they have much to prove, though. Smith ghosts around like he normally does, not really ever doing anything that you could put your finger on. He's a strange kind of a winger, because one place he never really appears is on the wing. Craig Noone is another of these 'anti-wingers', who is addicted to cutting inside all the time. Wingers are supposed to stay wide and create space, not come inside and minimise the space. He is normally on the right, so he can cut inside onto his favoured left foot. At Accy, it is more interesting, because he is on the left, so I think, 'Ah – I will get to see him go outside his marker today, like the old-fashioned wingers did.' Only – I don't. On the left, all Noone seems to do is try to cut inside people. Strange. Once or twice I see someone actually go on the outside and cross a ball on his left foot, only it always turns out to be the young left-back, who is actually a much better winger than Noone.

Up front, we have a retro-style 'little and large' pairing of Cornelius, our record signing from Denmark, and Nicky Maynard. When I say of Cornelius that he is our 'record signing from Denmark', I don't mean we paid more for him than anyone we had previously signed from Denmark. I mean that we paid more for him than anyone before, ever. And that he happens to be from Denmark. This point does need some clarification, especially after you have seen him play. He is a big bloke who sort of thrashes and lumbers about up front. City are attacking the far end in the first half, so he is a long way away, but he doesn't exactly look silky smooth. At one point, the ball is bouncing around in the Accy area, he tries to get control of it but can't, and ends up trying to shoot, hopelessly off-balance, and falls over. The shot goes off to near the corner flag, or somewhere. At this point, the lads in the home end, which is a noisy shed, are in hysterics, and are soon chanting the old favourite, 'Worra waste a money.' And I have to say, from where I am standing, seemingly with some justification.

Eventually Cornelius' game comes to an abrupt end when he goes down, and is stretchered off the pitch and straight into – this being Accrington Stanley – the car park. Rudy Gestede comes on, and now I am really worried about our 'great Dane', because we actually look a lot better when Rudy Gestede comes on. And Rudy Gestede was not really much of a player even in the Championship.

In the second half, we look better. Craig Conway comes on for Smith – another winger with something to prove. He proves nothing. Stuck on the right, he wants to cut inside all the time, and can't, because he can't use his left foot! So why not go outside the guy? What's wrong with these wingers these days? (Answer: they are one-trick ponies.) Eventually, Conway and Noone both being incapable of going outside anyone, they do the obvious and simply change wings.

City get 2 goals in 2 minutes to kill off the game. First, the ball comes in to Maynard, lurking near the edge of the area, from Declan John on the left. He flicks it over the head of the Accy defender, and then steers the ball clinically past the goalie – good goal. A minute later, the ball deflects off a defender into the path of Gestede, and he hits it, first time, into the back of the net. That looked quite good, too – well *done, Rudy! Maybe this guy is gonna do 'the big boys' some damage after all ... Oh, I should also say a word about the Accy fans. Despite the lack of numbers, they are fairly noisy. They have their own trademark song, which is sung to the tune of 'Anarchy in the UK'. It goes: 'I am a Stanley fan, I know just what I am ...' there are two indecipherable lines, and then it ends with: 'And I – want to be – Stanley.'*

Perhaps this can be adapted down the City?

Dear Diary,

Saturday, 31 August 2013

Cardiff City 0 – 0 Everton

k/o 3.00 p.m.

Back to basics then – another afternoon of hard graft in the Premier League. City, having done for Man. City, try the same tactics against Everton – defend, defend, defend, and hope to pinch a goal from somewhere. Everton have an awful lot of possession, and we are lucky that they didn't have the clinical finishing to punish us. Plus, Marshall pulled off a couple of crucial reaction saves. He is going to get plenty of practice this season, by the look of it!

Bellamy failed to score when Kim picked him out with a through ball which left 'Bellers' facing Tim Howard in a one-on-one in the first half. Instead of just dinking it past the keeper, which he might well have done instinctively a couple of years ago, he tried to go round him – but his first touch was woeful, and took him out towards the corner flag! Now Bellamy was one of those players a lot of people had down as a 'banker' to be good enough for this here Premier League. I don't like to be cruel, but it's starting to look like he's already past it at this level.

The crowd seemed happy with the draw, though. I suppose if you add the 1 point to the 3 we got against Man. City, then it's quite good. I mean, we would have taken 4 points from those two games at the start of the season. And there's another reason why a draw is really quite good. We won't be playing Everton every week.

Two

FOREVER AUTUMN

Dear Diary,

Monday, 2 September 2013

Fellow diarist Collins is off driving around Europe so I get the diary to myself for a while.

A few things have happened since the last game. First up, this 'transfer window' thing. The window is normally the pretext for a lot of hot air about which international superstars are going to be signed by which teams – who end up signing someone from Chesterfield instead. But, to be fair to Malky, he didn't rest on his laurels, he actually signed three players.

One was a young centre-back from Uruguay called Maxi Amondarain (no, it's not an anagram, that really is his name), who must be good, because he has played for the Uruguay Under-20 team. We can't get too het up about this one, though, because he is going straight into our 'development team'. So he is 'one for the future', as they say. (This normally means they end up playing for Newport County in three years' time.)The second was a right-back from France with an even stranger name: Kevin Theophile-Catherine.

Anyway, another question is why have we signed another right-back when we only signed John Brayford (a right-back, lest we forget) a few weeks ago? Now these first two signings might be described as 'speculative' and 'question-able'. The third one, though, is different: it is a player I have actually heard of. We have signed Peter Odemwingie from

West Brom. Now he has played in this here Premier League thingy before, and he has scored goals in it, too. With Odem-whatever-his-name-is, plus our mean defence, we could do some serious damage in this League. 17th place might be achievable after all.

Dear Diary

Friday, 6 September 2013

Next, we have had one of those infernal International breaks. I find them a pain in the arsenal. They used to have these games in midweek, leaving the Saturdays free for the serious stuff – league football.

Now what they do? They have 'double-headers', meaning one of the games is on the weekend. So the Premier League (and Championship) programme grinds to a halt, while we wait – with bated breath – for England's thriller in San Marino, and Wales taking on the might of the Faroe Islands. And then they go and put all these games on Friday night. So what happens on Saturday? Naff all, that's what. A total waste of a perfectly good Saturday. Who dreamed that nonsense up? Even worse than that, David Marshall (who already looks like he is gonna be our Player of the Season) is out injured after 'linking up with' the Scotland squad. Craig Bellamy is too – but that may be a blessing!

Dear Diary,

Saturday, 14 September 2013

Hull City 1 – 1 Cardiff City

k/o 3.00 p.m.

OK, so Hull. They are not Man. City, they are not Everton, they came up with us from the Championship. If you divide the Premier League into a top half and a bottom half, then they are definitely bottom half material. These are one of the teams we have to be looking at beating.

Hull make a good start. This geezer Aluko (whose sister plays for the England women's team – and yes, I have seen her play, I didn't just crib it from the paper!) wriggles about in the area and gets a shot in. Our second-string goalie, Joe Lewis, saves it, and the ball spoons up into the path of Hull's new striker, Danny Graham. Now he used to play for Swansea, so this situation has got 'goal' written all over it. But for some reason, he can't control the ball, and fires his shot harmlessly wide.

After this, City get on top and do something they have not done all season: they keep hold of the ball, and start spraying some passes around. For a good quarter of an hour, we are well on top. Then, just before half-time, it all goes to pot and Hull score a goal, out of the blue, from a corner. Hang on! That's the sort of goal we're supposed to score.

(Now this is our fourth game, and this is our third defensive blunder which has led to a goal. Left-back Andrew Taylor was AWOL when he should have been covering the near-post area. If he had been there, he would have cut out the cross before it came to Curtis Davies. Everyone is going on about our solid defending, but we have to cut out these errors – or we won't stay up.)

The second half gets underway. Now we know City are getting serious, because Don Cowie comes on. Me and a couple of mates have a tradition of having a bit of a laugh about the number of times Malky finds an excuse to bring Cowie on in games – if we are losing (to help us score!), if we are winning (to help us close the game down!), if we are drawing (to waste time!) – he can come on in any of those situations. Also, Cowie is one of our Scottish contingent, and he looks a bit like Malky, so we have a bit of a giggle about him being Malky's illegitimate offspring, like Gunner Graham and the sergeant major in It Ain't Half Hot Mum, *if you can remember that far back. Oh, and I should mention that none of us has ever quite understood what exactly Cowie does once he gets on the pitch.*

Now something amazing happens: Cowie comes on, and within 10 minutes, he looks like our best player. He breaks into space down the right, takes a pass and steers a perfectly weighted cross into the path of Whittingham, who hits a first-time volley into the net for our equaliser. Then, when Hull attack us, who is there with a crucial header out of play?

Cowie, that's who. I take back everything I ever said about the guy! And Malky knows a player when he sees one. City could have won it when Gunnarsson broke into the box, but when the cross came over, he couldn't control the header, and it went wildly over the bar. It's good that Gunnar is getting into the box, though. The game peters out in a draw.

Did we do enough to try and win it? Not really. Odemwingie was on the bench but never came on. I felt we were happy with the point. It's all very well drawing your away games as long as you win your homes. Well, that should be easy enough, 'cos it's Spurs at home next!

Dear Diary,
Wednesday, 18 September 2013

I is back! I have a beard but no sun tan.

This is all going to take a little getting used to again, mind. The Premier League seems to have abandoned the idea of midweek fixtures. That's a shame, isn't it? So instead of tuning in to follow our progress at Charlton or Peterborough, we have another blank week. Joe Ledley has a groin strain and misses Celtic's Champions' League tie, while the Jacks prepare for a crushing defeat in Valencia.

Dear Diary,
Saturday, 21 September 2013

This was always likely to happen, I guess.

Financial constraints during the summer, allied to the need to fund that extravagant drive across Europe, had prevented me from stumping up the cash needed to buy a season ticket. Oh that's OK, I thought, I can easily blag my way to some tickets on a match-by-match basis. After all, I am practically famous now, I am on the radio and everything.

Yeah, right.

So this Saturday morning at 8.00 a.m. I set off for the ticket office at our increasingly Premier League-looking ground to be first in the queue for the 800 or so new seats that the club had squeezed into various nooks and crannies around the stadium.

Despite a rolling, digital advertisement (like I say, Premier League) that declared the game to be a sell-out, I persevered and managed to grab a couple of girls from the ticket office in the car park. Lynsey assured me that there were random spaces still available, but it was going to cost me. I was first in when the space-age office opened, and made a beeline for said Lynsey.

'You have to become a member first, though,' she announced. '£30 – and there is only Silver Membership left now.'

I needed two tickets.

'That's two memberships,' announced Lynsey. '£60.' Even my Tremorfa maths could work that out.

'Do you have any seats together?' I desperately asked.

'Yeah. £40 each. No wait, here are two behind the goal, £30 each.'

There then followed a complicated series of transactions involving various pieces of plastic from my wallet, and piles of leaflets, brochures and similar plastic items passed through the glass by Lynsey. At no point did any item resembling an actual match ticket feature in this exchange, but Lynsey assured me that the two silver cards I now owned (one for me, one for son Dan) had stored the information on a chip within the card. Wow.

So there we are. I am £120 lighter, and out of the ground by 9.15 a.m., Dan will be elated. Lynsey has now entered my list of all-time favourite women at Number 7, just ahead of Pam, the battered old waitress from the former Patrice Restaurant in Clifton Street.

Dear Diary,

Sunday, 22 September 2013

Cardiff City 0 – 1 Spurs

k/o 4.00 p.m.

Now I more or less predicted this. Let's take a look at our home games so far. City were lucky to beat Man. City, given that we had minimal possession in that game – but we won.

We were pretty much outplayed by Everton, too – but we got a draw.

Now I could see we were lucky, and if we tried to do it the same way against Spurs, we would probably get nothing. But did Malky change the way we set up against Spurs? Do bears shit in woods?? And, yeah, you could make a case that we nearly won this one, too.

With 15 minutes to go, Odemwingie (more of whom later) pulled the ball back to the edge of the area, where Gunnarsson was unmarked – and Gunnar blasted the ball over the bar. If that had gone in, we probably would have won. Then our luck turned, and in stoppage time, a Spurs sub went up to the byline and seemed to have pulled it back behind Paulinho, but he managed to back heel it into the empty net. This is the Premier League, and these things happen. So yeah, we were 'unlucky'. The problem is that before Gunnar's chance, Marshall had already had to make about a dozen saves, including four or five really top-class stops, to keep us in it. If we had won – if we had got anything out of this game – would we have deserved it? No!

We have played five games now, and a pattern is emerging. All we are doing, really, is defending. We have signed Caulker, who is a quick defender, and he and big Ben Turner are a good match: but neither of them can pass the ball. We have signed Gary Medel, 'El Pit Bull' – why is a Chilean called 'Gary', by the way? – and he is a decent defensive midfielder, but now we have two of them, with him and Gunnar, and neither of them can pass the ball. So there is no build-up from the back. All that happens is that the ball mysteriously always goes to Turner, perhaps because he can kick it the furthest, and he hoofs it up field. To where our smallish lone striker, Fraizer Campbell, is standing – with a 6ft 3in brick outhouse centre-half right up his backside! We are just giving the ball back to the opposition and saying, 'come and have another go at us'. But in the Prem., if you keep doing that, they score.

And that's what happened today.

As for Gunnar's chance – yes, he gets into attacking positions, maybe once a game – but is Gunnar, who I see essentially as a tackling midfielder, the guy you want in those positions?

If you let the opposition have as many shots as we did today, is it really working having two defensive midfielders? Would we not be better off having a more creative one, so that we could keep the ball longer? That would be one way of restricting the other team's chances: keeping the damn ball ... There were signs, in the first 20 minutes, that the crowd are getting fed up with our essentially negative game.

However, there were two positive things to emerge from this match: Kevin Theo-Whatever is a real speed merchant at right-back, and can dart into dangerous positions; and Peter Odemwingie, within minutes of coming on for Campbell, showed that he is really capable of making a success of this lone striker role – and demonstrated, at the same time, that Campbell (too small, too slow to react to things) is not.

I feel a bit sorry for Campbell, because he has to toil like a headless chicken, running around after lost causes for an hour, and then – when another striker is ready to come on, who could help him out – he is hauled off! But Odemwingie, even on his own, is good. He is sharper, he is quicker to turn and face the goal, he knows who is around him – everything is a crucial split second quicker than it is with Campbell. I don't want to say anything big this early in the season, but – it could be that Odemwingie is the difference between going down and staying up!

Dear Diary,
Tuesday, 24 September 2013

The first of our prearranged planning sessions to discuss how the diary is taking shape. We have decided to use the International breaks as rough markers to break up the book. Dave thinks they represent punctuation marks in the season, but I just think they are good opportunities for a pint in Canton.

We aim for Wetherspoons on Cowbridge Road East, anticipating regular Sky TV updates on our cup clash at Upton Park. But the pub is only showing twenty-four-hour news, so we hear all about the crisis in Syria but little of City's embarrassing show, conceding a goal after 20 seconds. We eventually lose 3–2.

Good job this isn't a 'Secret Capital Cup Diary'.

Dear Diary,

Friday, 27 September 2013

Having turned down the chance to play for Wales, Ben Turner is now being spoken of as a possible England candidate.

Blimey, Dave, he is not exactly Larry Lloyd, is he?

Oh I dunno ... on his day perhaps.

Dear Diary,

Saturday, 28 September 2013

Fulham 1 – 2 Cardiff City

k/o 3.00 p.m.

Now I forgot to mention this, but after the Spurs game the previous Saturday, we had a big discussion in the pub, and I said maybe Jordon Mutch should be in the starting XI. Paul then informed me that last season, Mutch neither scored a goal for City, nor provided an assist. This information shocked me somewhat, but I said, surely Mutch was a better player on the ball than either Medel or Gunnarsson?

On the Tuesday, we played a reserve team against West Ham (Capital One Cup), and who was our Man of the Match (according to the Echo*)? Mutch, that's who. And he scored a goal. So I do get some things right.*

We lost the West Ham tie 3–2 away, and I will say no more about that.

More importantly, we were back to business in the League on the Saturday, playing a Fulham who had endured a poor start to the season. One sensed this could be the time to record our first away win. One sensed right! I was supposed to be getting a ticket off a friend of a friend of Peter Whittingham, but it was only a 'maybe', and it was too dodgy to go all the way to London on a wing and a prayer. So the pub it was.

There are now many pubs in town (Cardiff city centre) claiming to show all the City games live. But 'claiming' is the operative word. Last time around (Hull) it looked like the Queens Vaults couldn't get it, so I went to this downstairs place called Charlie Brown's. They had it on – big screens, too. This time, we all adjourn to the Borough, because it is 'supposed' to be on here. 'Supposed' being the operative word!

After fifteen minutes of fiddling around, it becomes clear that the Borough cannot get a 'stream' (I am told this is the proper technical term), and so we nip across St Mary Street in the hope that Charlie Brown's might have it. They do, but it is a fuzzy picture, and we end up going to the Vaults – who have it, clear as day, on a big screen. Hooray!

The business of finding a pub showing the game is probably the biggest suspense of the day. City are all over a poor Fulham side, dominating possession, and it is blindingly obvious that we will win. City duly take the lead after 12 minutes, Peter Whittingham's accurate corner – he is getting good at these – being headed home by Steven Caulker, as the statuesque Fulham defenders look on. City remain on top for some time after that, but cannot increase their lead. Then, out of nothing, just before half-time, Fulham midfielder Bryan Ruiz (who has just come on as a sub) conjures up a brilliant left-footed curler from outside the area that bends around Marshall – who can only watch it, even he is not superhuman – to land inside the far post: 1-1.

In the second half, Fulham get into it a bit more, and I start to wonder if this is going to end badly. It looks like a classic '1-0 up, 2-1 down' job. Then Mutch comes on. City immediately improve. Then, right at the death, the ball falls to Mutch off a defender's shoulder, just outside the box, and he suddenly fires a first-time, instinctive left-footed shot (his weaker foot) which loops over the Fulham keeper, David Stockdale, and into the net. The pub erupts in riotous merriment, I spill half my pint, but City have won their first away game of the season. I said it was obvious we would win! It's the first time since December 1961 that City have won an away game in the top division. The last time we did it was at Craven Cottage, too.

Oh, and we are definitely good enough to stay up – that is becoming obvious. It is clear to me after this game that City are going to finish at least in mid-table. That's pretty good going, isn't it? – it's still only September, and I don't have to worry about relegation any more.

Dear Diary,

Monday, 30 September 2013

I think we are getting the hang of this now.

In the olden days when Man United were above us in the League, all our opponents played at 3.00 p.m. on a Saturday afternoon. It was relatively easy to follow who was where, with only the odd 'high profile' game (AKA, ones where there might be trouble) such as Leeds v. Birmingham, to disrupt the fixture list.

But, as I say, we have the hang of it now. We celebrated with Kinnock-like fervour as City's great day at Fulham ended at 4.55 p.m., danced again as Rambo stuck it up the Jacks a few hours later and then watched *Match of the Day* three times, before Monday saw Everton topple our next opponents Newcastle, to leave us ... 11th in the League. What a weekend.

Dear Diary,

Tuesday, 1 October 2013

So, the real 'transfer window' closed some time ago but the 'loan window' is open today.

Of course, us Premier League clubs (still love saying that), are merely outside looking in, as we can only loan players out. Sadly this means that we didn't acquire Jack Collison from West Ham, who has now (amazingly ...) joined mighty Bournemouth, but it does allow us to unload Simon Lappin to Sheffield United.

As far as can be recalled, Lappin's only contribution to our cause seemed to be picking up a red card at Barnsley last season. Away games at Barnsley – seems a lifetime ago, doesn't it?

Dear Diary,

Thursday, 3 October 2013

Spent the morning stood on the touchline at the CCFC training venue out at the Vale Resort, hoping to persuade the lads to pose for a photo with my 'Happy Birthday Dan' sign ready for next week. (My son Dan's 21st birthday.) Sadly we were turfed out by security.

Sadly, the crumpled piece of paper we found discarded by Malky turned out to be his shopping list ... bargains he is looking for at Asda, not Arsenal unfortunately.

Dear Diary,

Saturday, 5 October 2013

Cardiff City 1 – 2 Newcastle United

k/o 3.00 p.m.

City are going down, no doubt about it. They are just not good enough. (Here we go again ...)

The problem is, we cannot keep possession.

Malky bases everything on a sound defence, and to be fair, nippy Steven Caulker and big Ben Turner, our two centre-backs, are both decent defenders at this level. But passing is neither one's strong suit. In front of them, we have two defensive midfielders – Gunnarsson and Medel – who don't seem too good at spraying the ball around either.

The away teams know this, and they hassle us remorselessly. At one point, Whittingham dropped back to help out, and he, Medel and left-back Andrew Taylor were all in close attendance, but three Newcastle attackers swarmed around them at once. The end result? The ball ended up going back to Big Ben – as it always mysteriously does – and he hoisted a high, hanging ball up field, for Fraizer Campbell, our lone striker, who seems to stand all of about 4ft 10in.

If we cannot keep possession for longer than ten seconds at a time (which we seemingly cannot), then what happens is, we keep giving it back to the opposition. And what happens then is that David Marshall has to make around 23 amazing saves every game, just to keep us in it. Marshall is already our 'Player of the Season' – the Supporters' Club might as well make the announcement now!

The only way we can resolve this problem is to be less negative. If the away teams are getting 23 shots per game, then clearly the 'safety-first' policy is not working. So we have to get rid of one of the defensive midfielders, and bring in a midfielder who can 'knock it about a bit', like Mutch. Again, Mutch came on, and we looked better for it. But the problem was, he came on when we were already 2-0 down.

Another weird thing that happens is that we seem to get more time on the ball in the second half. That is because these teams are not fit enough to play 'the pressing game' for 90 minutes. But the problem today was (sorry to be repetitive) we were already 2-0 down!

We managed to pull a goal back 10 minutes into the second half. Gunnarsson dispossessed a Newcy player and broke forward, then passed it to Mutch, who managed to lay it off, first time, to Peter Odemwingie, who had intelligently come off his right wing. Odemwingie kept his cool, evaded the first challenge by cutting inside, and calmly slotted the ball home. But 2-1 to them it remained.

Now this Odemwingie looks a good player, but he is no wide man, he is a central striker. You can tell he does not want to be out wide, and most of the time he abandons his role. This means more pressure on the right-back, Theophile, who also tends to wander up field and leave his post. This is how the first goal was conceded.

Fraizer cannot do a thing up front on his own. He will probably not score again all season in a lone striker role, other than maybe from another corner (where his only scores have come from). Odemwingie, though, might be able to score in this position.

Today, we were chasing the game at 2-0 down, and never once did Malky change from a lone striker policy. First we had hapless, helpless Fraizer – who is always off-balance – thrashing around up front on his own. Then he went off, Bellamy came on for him and played on the wing, and Odemwingie went up front – on his own. Then he went off and Nicky Maynard came on and played on his own.

This kind of negativity is criminal. We should play with two up front at times. But if we are going to play with one, it has to be Odemwingie, and not Fraizer Campbell.

Another thing that is clear is 'Bellers' has had it. No pace left. At one point, Whitts knocked the ball towards the space where Bellers should have been running, and he wasn't making the *run because he knows he can't get there anymore. He spends all his time running away from goal, instead of towards it. At times, he is getting in the way of Theophile, the right-back, who wants to get further up field than Bellers is willing to go. Keep him as a motivator on the bench by all means, Malky. Please don't waste a substitution by bringing him on again!*

Dear Diary,

Sunday, 6 October 2013

'Craig Bellamy to be the next Wales Manager!!' WTF ...??
(Memo to self: stop buying the *Wales on Sunday.*)

Dear Diary,

Tuesday, 8 October 2013

Despite the absence of midweek trips to the likes of Charlton and Peterborough, there remains plenty to keep the City fan interested on a Tuesday.

Take today – Craig Bellamy has confirmed his retirement from Wales duty after the next round of World Cup games; former City favourites Joe Ledley and Adam Matthews feature in a host of withdrawals from Chris Coleman's squad; and City fans in the Ninian Stand face a possible five game ban for persistent standing during matches. (How do Man. City fans get away with their famous Poznan routine if you can't stand up at Premier League games??)

Dear Diary,

Wednesday, 9 October 2013

Looks like another City old boy, James Collins, could come back on board for Wales after all. Wonder who blinked first?

Back at the CCS it seems we have a new 'Head of Recruitment' in place. Malky's trusted aide, Iain Moody, has been suspended and replaced by a 23-year-old from Kazakhstan, Alisher Apsalyamov.

I'll need to upgrade my spell checker at this rate.

Three

FIREWORKS

Dear Diary,

Thursday, 10 October 2013

What was that line about 'going viral'?

Yesterday's throwaway line about a backroom reshuffle has become national news.

Turns out this new recruitment guy has little or no football knowledge, had only been with the club on work experience doing bits and pieces of painting (??) and is some sort of mate of Tan's son, Eugene. Moody was told in writing at 2.00 p.m. yesterday that he had been suspended, over some alleged shenanigans in the summer transfer window, but by 6.00 p.m. this had been reduced to 'gardening leave'.

The result of this has shifted the world on its axis. The promotion of the work experience kid is said to have 'painted Malky into a corner' *(groan)* while, for the first time in my lifetime we have made the front page of the *Sun*. Cardiff City Trust Chairman Tim Hartley is even quoted in today's *Guardian*.

This shambles followed some sort of spat between the players and the owner over bonus payments, which apparently led to the players demanding that Tan be banned from the dressing room. Has Moody been made a scapegoat here?

I haven't even set off for work as I write this, but already today there are stories and rumours flying around with suggestions that Malky has been asked to resign, and reminders that the high-trousered one's previous antics include an attempt to recruit Alan Shearer as City manager. You might be forgiven for thinking that any of this was actually happening at all to be honest, as Jason Perry (in the *Daily Mirror*) points out to Tan that 'this isn't PlayStation!'

Message boards, etc. are in meltdown over this as you can imagine, but, as if we needed any reminding, Radio Wales have described Vincent Tan as a man 'who doesn't have a history of listening to fans' opinions'. You're telling me.

At least we have a quiet time ahead on the field as Bonfire Night looms. Our next three games are Chelsea away, Norwich City and ... Swansea City.

Dear Diary,
Friday, 11 October 2013

Me: 'Looks like you could be getting a new manager for your birthday at this rate, Dan.'
Dan: 'Can't I just have a bike or something?'
Me: 'We don't always get what we want in this life, son.'

Dear Diary,
Saturday, 12 October 2013

The diarists meet to discuss latest developments at the club:
'So Gareth, how do you reckon the summer signings are doing?'
'Not great, Dave, not great.'
'But look at the big names we grabbed – Medel, Cornelius ...'
'Well, Medel has done okay, perhaps, but the big Dane is always injured.'
'So you aren't impressed by the work of our scouting team yet then?'
'Jeez Dave, I got a mate who is a painter and decorator who could have done a better job.'

Dear Diary,

Sunday, 12 October 2013

No Premier League action today thanks to the Internationals, so I decide on some retail therapy with a trip into town. Wandering around HMV, I discover that Goldie Lookin' Chain's new album is entitled 'Kings of Caerleon'.

Priceless.

Happy 21st Birthday

Dan

Tuesday, 15 October 2014.

Dear Diary,

Tuesday, 15 October 2013

Finally, the eagerly awaited board statement following yesterday's meeting at the Cardiff City Stadium.

We understand that Malky has not resigned but seems to have been given some sort of dreaded 'vote of confidence'. Other actions to emerge from the five-hour meeting include the establishment of committees to look at nomination & corporate governance, audit, health & safety and the development of the stadium. Yippee! The club is a national laughing stock and they respond with a health & safety committee.

We had to wait until gone 5 o'clock to learn all this, mind – before that the website was content to concentrate on Craig Bellamy's last game for Wales tonight away in Belgium.

Apparently all this began because Tan believed Mackay had overspent during the summer – but who was signing the cheques? So Tan says to Dato to tell Lim to instruct Malky to remind Moody not to spend more than £20 million ... And he forgets, in the meantime, that Dato isn't there anymore, because he has already replaced him with Dalman. What a way to run a business!

Dear Diary,

Friday, 18 October 2013

At the end of a car crash week for Cardiff City, I met up with Sian from Bluebirds Unite this evening. Sian is always pretty feisty, but there was simply no stopping her tonight.

Sian led an emotional discussion, which ranged from the rebranding, the bonus row and rumours about Tan's meddling in team affairs, to the shadowy role of Sam Hammam and the lack of any real depth to the press statement ...

Look What they've Done to my Song, Ma.

Dear Diary,

Saturday, 19 October 2013

Chelsea 2 – 1 Cardiff City

k/o 3.00 p.m.

City have endured a bad couple of weeks since the last game (at home to Newcastle).

First the story of unpaid bonuses, and chairman Vincent Tan not being 'welcome' in the dressing room as a result. Then, within days of this story breaking, there was that even worse one, involving the suspension and then dismissal of Malky Mackay's trusted henchman, Iain Moody, and his replacement by the 23-year-old Kazakh lad.

However, everything is now OK, because we have had the obligatory five-hour board meeting (on Monday), and Malky has more or less been given the familiar 'vote of confidence' (although nobody has used this exact term). And we all know what happens after that ...

I suppose it's just as well we are away to Chelsea after all this chaos, as we would not have expected anything from this game in any case.

The game was to be viewed in another pub. After the week we have just had, I cannot afford to risk watching this game sober.

City make changes, with Odemwingie now playing in the striker's role (instead of Fraizer Campbell) – just as I had advised Malky! Don Cowie therefore plays in Odem's old place on the right – another good move. And Jordon Mutch starts (another good change), but for Kim, meaning we still have the two defensive midfielders, Medel and Gunnarsson. I think maybe Mutch should have come in for one of them – although it is hard to see us ever dropping Medel, as we have paid so much for him.

After only a few minutes' play, Marshall boots the ball up field, and Odemwingie – who always manages to have some kind of effect upon the play, unlike Campbell, who very rarely does – uses his body to shield the ball from his marker, John Terry, who can do nothing to stop the flick-on. It seems harmless, but it has gone into a dangerous area.

Another defender (Ramires) taps it back towards goal, perhaps to David Luiz, perhaps to Petr Cech – who knows? And who cares? All we care about is the fact that Luiz leaves it to Cech, and does not even worry about the fact that Mutch is now charging towards the goal. The ball slows up in the wet, and doesn't reach Cech. Mutch gets there an instant before him, and seemingly without thinking about it, he instinctively nicks it over the keeper and into the empty net. So two of our new starters have combined to create a goal: 1–0 City. Keep feeding the monkeys!

For a while, Chelsea look quite ordinary. Odemwingie gets the better of Terry again in another tussle, and from the free-kick, Whitts finds Odemwingie, whose flicked header is turned around the post only by an acrobatic save from Cech.

If we had scored another goal, things might have looked quite interesting. But no – Marshall gets dispossessed by Samuel Eto'o whilst bouncing the ball (apparently illegally, although none of us realised that at the time), and the ball ends up being bundled into the back of the net by Hazard (Eden, not Mickey!): 1–1. A pity that this one was given, as Chelsea do not really need any help from the officials to overcome Cardiff City!

We decamp to the Borough for the second half. This time the Borough does have the game – but as the half progresses, it also has more and more Cardiff Blues rugby supporters, who are marching in for a pint at the end of their Heineken Cup win over Toulon (at the stadium just across the road). This is the first time City and Blues fans have been forced by the fixture schedules to 'coexist' in one crammed pub – interesting!

Back to the match – in the second half, class begins to tell, although some of the goals seem to be repeat goals of ones we have conceded against other teams. The first one (after 66 minutes) was just a bit of class from Hazard, hovering between the halfway line and the edge of our box. He came inside his marker and looked up – and this is the area where teams like Chelsea have the quality to really hurt you, and teams like Cardiff don't. Hazard played the killer ball between defenders into another space, into which Eto'o had moved; and Eto'o had simply to evade one challenge (from Caulker), cut inside and slot the ball between Marshall and the near post. 2–1 to Chelsea, and they did make that one look childishly simple.

If only we could do the same ... Difficult to pinpoint who, if anyone, was at fault for that one.

The next one began with a weak header from left-back, Andrew Taylor, which nevertheless could have been dealt with by Gunnarsson; however, he was beaten to it by the quicker thinking Ramires, and the ball broke to Oscar. Three City defenders all backed off him, wondering which way he was going to turn; and after a couple of twists, he simply drilled the ball into the net. Somebody somewhere had to pile in and make a meaningful challenge!

The 4th goal was the 'repeat'. Theophile was missing at right-back, and Caulker went over to cover (just as happened against Newcastle). Caulker does not seem too hot when he gets pulled into this position; as against Newcastle, he was unable to prevent the guy (Hazard again) from cutting inside, even though it was fairly obvious that the Belgian would try to do so. On this occasion, the shot was a mere daisy-cutter, but Marshall compounded the problem by letting the ball slip gently past him – probably because he was still 'psyched out' by the goal he had conceded in the first half.

Having said that, even before that goal, Marshall was lucky to 'get away with one', when he chanced his arm by catching the ball outside his area. A ropey afternoon all round, then, for the Scotsman – but at least he has made all his mistakes in the one game, and in a game which we probably would have lost anyway!

Conclusions: Theophile goes missing at right-back. Caulker is weak when he has to cover across in the right corner. Marshy had been on the Scotch the night before (joke)!

We look better with Mutch in the team, but do we really need Gunnarsson and Medel? 'Gunnar' got forward again today once, as he does every game – but did nothing with his header. He is no good in those situations, and he is also getting caught in possession a lot.

We therefore need Mutch (not Gunnar) and Medel in front of the defence, and Kim as the attacking midfielder (Kim almost scored with a cross-shot after coming on as a sub). As Malky now seems ready to change things, perhaps he will adopt this formation at Norwich in a week's time.

The problem is, I think we really need to get something at Norwich. It seems to me that if we lose there, that could be the pretext for Chairman Tan to get rid of Malky. Difficult to believe, but there you are.

It's a hard world in this Premier League thingy.

Dear Diary,
Sunday, 20 October 2013

FAO all goalkeepers out there:
   Why do you feel the need to bounce the ball prior to kicking it?
   I mean, why do you do that, eh?
   (We will also accept answers from tennis players.)

Dear Diary,
Wednesday, 23 October 2013

I see Wills and Kate didn't pick José Mourinho as one of the godparents for George's christening today. They'll be sorry.

The row over the ball-bouncing goal seems to have been replaced by 'The Special One's' latest rantings over Cardiff City's 'time-wasting' tactics at Stamford Bridge. He wittily claimed that City fans pay for 90 minutes, but only see about 55 minutes of actual play.

Funny that, I don't recall the ref adding on 35 minutes of stoppage time last Saturday. I wonder how he will set his game plan up if he needs to win the last game of the season against us. If Chelsea are 1–0 will he push on for more goals, I wonder? We shall have to see.

Dear Diary,
Friday, 25 October 2013

Here's one for you ...
   I wrote this e-mail to well-known City fan Neil Kinnock today:

   Dear Lord Kinnock,
   As you know, the clocks go back this weekend as BST draws to a close.

I wondered, would it be possible for you to use your good offices to persuade the powers that be to turn the clocks back to the time when Mr Vincent Tan made his regrettable decision to change the famous blue shirts of Cardiff City to red? This would give Mr Tan the opportunity to reverse a decision which has proved so unpopular.

Would that be in your gift, I wonder?

To be fair to him, Lord Kinnock actually replied. We are unable to reproduce the full reply in these pages, but he thanked me for my 'interesting suggestion'. Whilst not being a particular fan of the rebranding, Lord Kinnock seemed more concerned with the recent disposal of Iain Moody, referring to his concerns at anything which materially affected the team's performances.

Wow, thanks Neil.

Dear Diary,

Saturday, 26 October 2013

Norwich City 0 – 0 Cardiff City

k/o 3.00 p.m.

City have had some tough games at home (Man. City, Everton, Spurs), and a tough one away (Chelsea). Now we have a 'winnable' game – away to Norwich, who are one of the few teams below us. Does 'winnable' mean we can actually win it?

I decide to do something traditional for this game – listen to it on the radio. This will give me a different perspective to seeing it on a screen at a crowded pub. I can listen to the comments of the commentator (not Robert Phillips, some other guy), and the pundit, who this week is City's well-loved former defender Jason 'Psycho' Perry – who usually talks some sense, I feel.

Now, Malky is slowly changing things round a bit. He has already brought Mutch into the starting XI, as I 'advised' him to do. Now he is going a stage further, and starting with Mutch and Kim, which means Gunnarsson is 'rested', and we only have one defensive midfielder (Medel), rather than two – as I also suggested he do. (Hey, this management game is not rocket science, you know.) The only problem now is that he has rested Cowie, and now has Odemwingie on the right wing – where he does not really want to be – and Fraizer Campbell (completely ineffectual) as the lone striker.

So what happens?

What happens is that we get overrun by Norwich's five-man midfield, and are dominated for most of the match. Although Mutch has one chance early on, which Norwich keeper, John Ruddy, manages to save, that is all that City create all afternoon. The rest is all Norwich, and City only hang on for the draw because our old friend David Marshall pulls off his usual quota of about 7 startling saves.

There is a kerfuffle at the end because some Dutch berk of a Norwich midfielder (the strangely named Leroy Fer) decides to knock the ball into the empty net, instead of passing it back to Marshall, after we have kicked the ball out so that their injured player can be treated. It looks like a goal, in the final minute of play, but luckily the ref (Mike Jones) found a pretext to disallow the goal, claiming he hadn't blown for the throw to be taken.

(Since the importation of foreign players in large numbers over the past 20 years, we have seen a large increase in instances of cheating. And here was another example of it. Discuss.)

Anyway, the 'goal' did not stand, and we got away with a 0–0 draw. But this was a 'winnable' game, and we were outplayed once again. So what did the game tell us?

We were overrun in midfield. Playing Medel, Mutch and Kim did not work – too lightweight. Again, we could not keep the ball for any length of time. But Jason Perry made an interesting point – every time Medel had the ball, the Norwich players took this as a signal to swarm around him and pressurise City in their own half. Now, this Medel character cost us £9 million or whatever, and he seems to be a guy who can make a couple of tackles. He keeps getting 7 out of 10 in the newspaper reports (in The Times, *I mean – the* Echo *gives everybody 7 or 8 regardless!), but the opposition know he is weak on the ball, and harry him as soon as he has it. Like I said earlier, Malky won't drop him because he paid so much for him, but is Medel becoming our weak link? Should we have dropped him instead of Gunnarsson? Discuss.*

While Psycho's comments made my doubts about Medel even bigger, he did contradict me on the subject of Fraizer Campbell. Psycho likes Campbell, because of his work rate, and because he thinks City lack somebody to play 'the killer ball' behind the defence for Fraizer to latch on to. In fact, Odemwingie played a 'killer ball' through to him, resulting in the Mutch chance. But often Fraizer does not get any such ball throughout the game. So with our current formation, is there any point playing him? Discuss.

At half-time, Malky acted decisively, bringing on Cowie (better defensively down the right) and Gunnarsson. But he left Fraizer on and took off Odemwingie – even though Odemwingie is far better in the lone striker role than Fraizer ...

Looking at the bigger picture, the draw kept us above Norwich, so we are still not in the bottom three (yet). We got a point, so we now have 9 points from 9 matches, so we still have the required 1 point per game ratio to stay up (just). But you look at the 'leading scorers' column, and we have nobody – Fraizer is still our leading scorer with 2, which was what he had after the opening week of the season!

And we were the last game on Match of the Day, *on which Gary Lineker said it was too early to call the game a 6-pointer. But he was just being polite! Conclusion: City are, to use a technical term, 'in the shit'.*

Dear Diary,
Sunday, 27 October 2013

Well that was a weird one, wasn't it? I also went for the traditional approach for yesterday's game – choosing the traditional wireless over the wonders of Albanian satellite TV or wherever it is that the Queens Vaults obtain their pictures from.

I sat in Waitrose car park listening to the dying embers of what had been a pretty uninspiring outing by the sound of things. *(Waitrose??? I think the publishers must be paying you too much, Dave.)* As the final moments ebbed away I even found myself counting out the last minute of added time in an attempt to make the seconds pass more quickly. Why do we engage in this type of thing, eh? It's right up there with wearing your lucky socks, isn't it, on the 'List of pointless actions' pile? Crazy thinking. (Memo to self: remember to wear lucky socks to Jacks game.)

Anyway, as the seconds had ticked away, I entered that surreal world of hearing the other team 'score' but heard no cheers from the home fans. To me it sounded like the goal should stand, but the ref found some loophole in the laws about not having blown the whistle and made Norwich take that throw-in again. Do refs have to blow before a throw-in these days??

If Norwich get relegated on goal difference that could be a bit awkward. Mind you, if they couldn't score properly against us in a game like yesterday, then goal difference is the least they have to worry about if you ask me.

Dear Diary,
Monday, 28 October 2013

Well, it's started.

Wall-to-wall coverage on the radio. Message boards overrun, TV trailers and a special BBC documentary on telly tonight.

The derby is approaching. Light the blue touch paper, and retire.

Dear Diary,
Tuesday, 29 October 2013

For a reason I find difficult to comprehend, elements of the local media seem especially animated over the appointment of the referee for Sunday's derby – Mike Dean. This seems to have especially caught the imagination of our friends down west, with one local website 'The Swansea Way' describing his appointment today as 'a completely ridiculous appointment for the South Wales derby'. The site describes how Dean had 'bowed to crowd pressure in the last fixture to be contested between Cardiff & Swansea and shouldn't have been appointed'.

Blimey ...

Mike Dean refereed the game between the two rivals at Ninian Park four years ago and was struck by a coin from the Bob Bank. (Incidentally, to those who edit that 'Swansea Way' site, this game was not the 'last fixture' between the clubs. We have played you several times since.) Anyway, Dean also awarded a somewhat soft penalty in the dying seconds of that game – which Ross McCormack gleefully struck away just yards from my seat at the front of the Canton Stand.

Is all this likely to worry him now and affect his judgement? Will he be swayed if Bellers goes down in the box late in the game on Sunday, giving Whitts a chance to complete his hat-trick from the spot?

Let's hope so, eh?

Dear Diary,

Thursday, 31 October 2013

More City players go out on loan for the experience. Kadeem Harris has been hitting the heights at Brentford, we hear, and now young Oshilaja has driven down the M4 to join Newport Cewnty – assuming he is old enough to drive, that is. We now have Nugent, McNaughton, Ralls, Conway, Harris, Lappin and Oshilaja out on loan. Amazingly, though, we still have Kiss and Velikonja at the club.

Oshilaja even scored for his new club in the Johnstone's Paint Trophy last night against Pompey.

Yes ... that Pompey.

Dear Diary,

Friday, 1 November 2013

On a busy news day in South Wales, we learn that Leighton James believes that few, if any, of the City side would get into the Swansea XI; the decision to sign Etien Velikonja was taken without Mackay's blessing; and our new 'head of recruitment', Alisher Apsalyamov, has temporarily been suspended from his duties after being investigated by Home Office officials regarding his work permit!

In other news, David Cameron has announced a referendum on tax-raising powers for the Welsh Assembly, the M4 Relief Road looks like it could be financed through borrowing, and Barack Obama is coming to Newport next year for the NATO summit.

I hope he has his work permit.

Dear Diary,

Saturday, 2 November 2013

I don't like it when City don't have a game on Saturday. The whole focal point of the day seems absent somehow. Let's see how our rivals are doing though.

Strewth, Norwich get tonked 7–0 by Man. City!! This is a good thing, yeah? It's worth a point to us for the goal difference, and the more teams like Norwich, Crippled Paralysis and Sunderland become cast adrift the better for us.

As long as none of them try and pinch our manager.

Dear Diary,

Sunday, 3 November 2013

Cardiff City 1 – 0 Swansea City

k/o 4.00 p.m.

Now, this is confusing. Whenever the London papers need a shorthand term for City they call us 'the Welsh team'. You know how it works in journalism: in the first paragraph of the story, it will say something like 'Cardiff are set to part company with their manager, Malky Mackay'. Then the next paragraph will say something akin to 'the Welsh team have made a decent start to the season, but tensions have arisen between Mackay and the club's owner Vincent Tan'. So we are 'the Welsh team'.

Now I find out that there is another team from Wales who are also in this Premier League thing. They are also sometimes referred to as 'the Welsh team'. So there are actually two Welsh teams in the Prem. You can see why I am disconcerted.

Another reason I am 'disconcerted' is because some guy I know in Swansea, who is known to my circle of friends as 'Gary the Jack', texted me after we beat Man. City in our opening home game of the season. Now this lad, Gary, has worked as a football scout, so I was expecting some fairly relevant comment from him. But all he said was, 'you're still going down'.

Okay, we have established that this is an important match. A really, really important one.

It actually begins just like all our other home games this season: City on the defensive, unable to keep hold of the ball, seeming to invite the visiting team to have it back and attack us. After 20 minutes, I am getting a bit fed up of it. On the plus side, Swansea don't actually look like scoring. On the minus side, my feeling is that if you keep giving the other team the ball, they will score sooner or later. And the less your own team has it, the less likely that you are gonna score.

Something has changed, though. Bellamy is back and playing on the left (Don Cowie is on the right), which means that Peter Whittingham is now playing through the middle, where he has more influence on the game. Whitts is coming back to take the ball out of the defence, and helping out Medel, who normally struggles in this department. Sometimes even Jordon Mutch, our 'attacking' midfielder, is coming back to offer a variation. We lose the ball a few times, but we stick at it, and after those first nervy 20 minutes, we start doing something we have seldom managed at home: we start stringing some passes together.

It is goalless at half-time, but in the second half, we seem to get on top. Swansea, when they have the ball, don't do much with it. It's the first game for a while in which Marshall doesn't have to pull off 10 big saves. Then, midway through the second half, we get a corner, Bellers whips it in, and Caulker rises above everyone to nod it into the Swansea net: 1-0 City.

Swansea try to come back at us, but again, they do not look like scoring. Odemwingie – restored to the lone striker role – goes off, and Fraizer Campbell comes on. This is a bad move, as Campbell cannot hold onto the ball. But with the game entering stoppage time (5 minutes of it! Where did that come from?!),

Campbell shows that pace can sometimes be an asset when the other team are 'chasing the game'. A long through ball gets him in behind the Swansea defence, and the keeper – the curiously named Vorm – takes him out. Vorm is, inevitably, sent off. Swansea have had their three substitutions, so full-back Rangel has to go in goal. And by the time all this has been sorted out and the ref has got their wall to retreat for the free-kick, 3 of the 5 added minutes have been wasted. Lovely stuff!

Swansea finally get the ball back, but it is too late. The final whistle has blown and City have won 1-0. We retire to the pub for post-match analysis.

This went along the lines of: Medel is actually brilliant. What was I on about, suggesting he was a weak link? He was our best player! (Okay, maybe I got this wrong. So I will retract and admit: Medel is brilliant. Okay?) City are now 12th, and we are not struggling at all, we are a mid-table side. (So maybe I got that wrong, too. Maybe I'm getting a lot of things wrong. It's a confusing time.)

Hang on, though, I'm getting a text message from Gary the Jack, so this should help clear up the confusion. Did I mention he used to be a football scout? I read it in keen anticipation. It says: 'you're still going down'.

Dear Diary,

Sunday, 3 November 2013

(Again!)

All roads lead to the pub to savour the post-match glories of this November afternoon. Rain everywhere. Thirsts to die for. A sea of blue, by the way.

The pub is noisy in the extreme, though that barely registers as we find our usual cronies and usual corner. As the mood settles, Gareth and I ponder the season so far. Ten games in; a quarter of the season. 'Judge me after ten games,' they always say.

Okay then. We will ...

What I have learnt after ten games: Kevin Theophile-Catherine, our right-back, is good going forward and his defensive side has improved, too. If there is space, he will run into it, and then look to find a teammate. If there is a simple ball 'on' up the wing for Cowie, he will play it simple. On the other side, Andrew Taylor, our left-back, is nowhere near as good. If he is given the ball going into space, he gets a 'nosebleed' and wants to get rid of it. He doesn't cross it much, he doesn't get outside or beyond the defenders much, and he often chooses the wrong pass, and gives it to someone (today, to Bellamy) when they are already marked, meaning we just get stuck in a 'box' on the left side of the pitch. At some point, we need to discover a better left-back. Is the teenager, Declan John, ready yet? He is a converted winger, so he may be better on the ball. And although that may leave us open defensively, Taylor is not brilliant in that department, either, he often fails to spot an obvious 'runner' darting into his channel.

Hmm, I think you are being a bit 'glass half empty' there to be honest, Gareth. The back five has a settled look to it and has kept two consecutive clean sheets. Medel was awesome today doing the spade work – keeping possession via a series of short passes. Turner has developed the knack of 'playing percentages' (i.e. he boots it into the stand when needed). Marshall is making brilliant saves every game. *(Turner boots it all the time!!)*

We have cover at the back and options in midfield. *(We have too many midfield players, Dave!)* We may have been lucky to escape the odd hiding here and there this season (Spurs?) but … ten games in = 12 points. I will take that.

Fraizer Campbell is definitely better coming on as a sub – running against tired legs – than starting the game. If we play one striker, we have to start with Odemwingie. But I have said this already. Medel, Whitts and Mutch is our best midfield combination. We have to keep Whitts in the middle. But this raises the question of who plays on the left when Bellers doesn't play? To which my answer is, Kim? Yes, he doesn't come back to defend much, but if he is playing outside (and ahead of) Whitts, then Whitts can do some of the covering for him.

My midfield would be:

Medel

Cowie   Whitts   Kimbo   Bellers

I am reserving my judgement on who is best to sit up top until Cornelius is fit. I don't see Odemwingie as the answer there. He always seems to drift out wide, ending up crossing the ball to where he himself should be. I like Campbell.

I also like the rumour that City are linked with Wilfried Zaha, the ex-Palace lad now at Man. Utd. Pace and talent out wide. We have missed real pace since the days of Chris Burke to be honest.

Anyway Gareth, get the beers in. My glass is half empty here ...

Dear Diary,

Monday, 4 November 2013

I knew I was being optimistic. The rigours of yesterday proved too much for me and I was home from work by 3 ... and asleep on the sofa by 4.

I resurfaced just in time for BBC Wales' news, which was well worth watching this evening, as you might expect.

The bus back into town had been absolutely mental yesterday by the way – Ely to town, and they are all 'excited'. Endless renditions of the new Gary Medal/Kimbo chant, complete with ludicrous actions. Rest assured, I joined in unreservedly.

This is why we watch football. So we can dance on buses when it goes well.

Four

AFTER THE
GOLD RUSH

Dear Diary,
Tuesday, 5 November 2013

As the euphoria of last weekend's heroics relents, a strange feeling of unease appears to have descended around all who follow the fortunes of Cardiff City AFC.

Nathan Blake (who is emerging as a pundit of some credibility, I would argue) captured the mood in yesterday's *Echo*. For, despite the glee of a famous victory, and a respectable tally of 12 points from ten games, we still watch anxiously as Malky and Tan enter something of a 'Cold War'. Like miserable parents on the verge of divorce, they only seem to be staying together for the benefit of children at the moment. We just know that any divorce proceedings would result in Tan winning custody of the kids and keeping the house on Sloper Road. Malky would find himself a new lover in, I dunno, East Anglia or somewhere miles away. We would get to see him twice a year, if we were lucky.

These should be such happy times but, despite, or maybe, because of, Tan's millions, the future looks ... uncertain at best.

Dear Diary,
Wednesday, 6 November 2013

You can tell there is an International break looming. Managers are dropping like flies as the 'managerial merry-go-round' cranks into gear. Chris Hughton is hanging on tightly as we speak. 'Others' may be watching as the roundabout turns uneasily. West Ham on Saturday could be his last chance to avoid slipping off.

We learn today that John Hartson has hopped off the merry-go-round for now and stood down from his post with Wales. Never quite sure what his role was with Wales, to be honest, something to do with the lone striker role apparently, but the 'rumour mill' (why are these matters so ridden with clichés?) would have us believe that he could be about to form a 'dream team' (there's another ...) with Chris Coleman at Palace. Looks like they may be seeking inspiration from the Republic of Ireland, who have similarly appointed Martin O'Neill and Roy Keane in answer to the Irish Question.

Martin O'Neill for Chris Coleman. Is that really like-for-like, I wonder? It's not looking good for Palace if the answer to their question is 'Chris Coleman and John Hartson'.

Dear Diary,
Thursday, 7 November 2013

All a bit quiet on the CCFC front today. No bad thing after all the recent histrionics, perhaps.

(Dave – did you not see The Times *today? Their football writer was reviewing the top of the Premier League thingy. He says that Man. Utd have some 'tough' games ahead, including Arsenal, Cardiff away and Spurs. Proof that we have 'arrived!' We are now (at least at home) a 'tough' fixture. The new Stoke!)*

We learn today that Martin Atkinson will referee our forthcoming clash away at Villa. It's the first time he's officiated a City game since our 2–0 Carling Cup win over Blackburn Rovers in 2011 on our way to the final. He has issued 32 yellow cards so far this season and no red cards. Gary Medel, please take note.

Looking back through the archives it seems that his first time in charge of a City game was the 2–1 FA Cup defeat at Highbury against Arsenal in 2006. I was at that game – I think it was the last FA Cup tie played at Highbury, though I may be wrong on that. Answers on a postcard to ...

Our team that day included Jeff Whitley, Kevin Cooper, Neal Ardley and Neil Cox. Arsenal fielded Bergkamp, Van Persie and Robert Pires – who appeared to play in slippers. Amazingly, we kept the score down to a single goal defeat. Whether we can manage that in a few weeks' time, when we next play Rambo's lot, is another matter.

Dear Diary,
Friday, 8 November 2013

The Times mentions City for the second day running. Today we are the answer, in the daily general knowledge quiz, to the question 'Who did Aaron Ramsey play for before he joined Arsenal?' Yes I know it's only a quiz question, but this is evidence that we are seeping into the consciousness of Middle England. We are becoming a feature of the national sports scene.

Cardiff City Supporters' Trust official, Phil Nifield, put in a guest appearance on the Cardiff City phone-in tonight. Phil gave the listeners chapter and verse on the forthcoming '1993 Promotion Party' at the Cardiff City Stadium. The trust have lined up a host of names from those great days – Blakey, Pikey, Searley ... should be one for the purists to really enjoy. *(What about Brazily and Richardsony?)*

I have been asked to knock up a quiz for the 'half-time' entertainment. So far I have 'Against which country did Jason Perry win all of his international caps?' That should set the right tone, eh?

STOP PRESS: FELLOW RADIO HOST, 'GIGGSY', COLLARED ME AFTER THE SHOW TO ANOUNCE THAT HE HAS A SPARE TICKET GOING FOR THE VILLA GAME AND 'DID I WANNA GO???' HIS PLAN IS THAT IF I DRIVE HE WILL SORT ME OUT WITH A TICKET IN THE DOUG ELLIS STAND. YOU GOT YOURSELF A DEAL, GIGGSY.

Dear Diary,

Saturday, 9 November 2013

(Cue here, change of match reporter for the day …!)

Aston Villa 2 – 0 Cardiff City

k/o 3.00 p.m.

So 10.00 a.m. finds the Collins' Peugeot 206 outside Chez Giggsy as planned.

Giggsy makes a not-entirely-unexpected jibe at my 'hairdresser's car' before devoting the next 20-odd miles to analysing my CD collection. He is twenty-five years my junior and works for a radio show. I nervously await his verdict. Giggsy is a proper DJ. He talks of 'banging tunes', 'dance anthems' and 'drum and bass'. He 'works the clubs' and is 'all over Twitter'.

Gareth would be lost with this guy.

Anyway, he seems reasonably impressed that my collection features such 'Old Skool' acts as The Fugees and Soul to Soul. He also shows 'nuff respect' at the sight of an Ella Fitzgerald album. He is less impressed by my twelve Rod Stewart CDs, and unmoved by Cyndi Lauper. He has never heard of Frankie Valli & the Four Seasons.

I choose the scenic route to Villa via the M50 and M5. We reach a large tavern deep in the middle of England. Giggsy gets the beers in as I clutch my single Budweiser. All is well with the world.

Villa Park is a proper football ground. It is majestic. Like a stately home bedecked in claret and blue. Our brave boys receive a hero's welcome from the travelling support, still basking, no doubt, from Derby Day. We spot a large banner: 'In Malky We Trust'.

The occasion saw one of those almost surreal moments at a football ground as, prior to kick-off, all 35,809 spectators stood in silence in tribute to those who had fallen in conflict. The two minutes' silence, in advance of Remembrance Sunday tomorrow, was observed impeccably, before the shrill peep of Mr Atkinson' s whistle brought an almighty roar of expectation from all parts of the stadium.

Much like last week's performance, the first half was largely uneventful. Villa hadn't managed a goal for weeks and our centre-half is our top scorer. We could see this game slipping further and further down the *Match of the Day* scheduling as the first 45 minutes ended. Still, no matter, City had rarely been troubled and the home fans had started to get on the backs of the Villa. A good sign. We had even almost taken the lead with what would have been a headed own goal. Couldn't quite make out the culprit from where we were, sorry.

The second half was a brighter affair, with City pressing forward more, Bellers looking interested and Whitts fancying his luck here and there. We also saw a very, very strong penalty claim rejected after Caulker was pulled about in the box *(ooh errr!)* We certainly saw softer penalties than that given this weekend, didn't we, José? Worrying signs as Gunnars goes off with a recurrence of that shoulder injury, though.

Now Giggsy and I were commenting on the phone-in last night about how Medel, for all his 'pit bull' image, has yet to pick up a booking this season. Indeed, Cardiff City had conceded the least number of fouls in the top flight, we remarked.

Well, what were we thinking? Cometh the hour, of course, cometh the man. Dear Pit Bull chose today to commit his most childish foul of the season with a piece of shirt tugging that would have got me a right smack if I'd tried it on the Cardiff parks a few years ago. The Chilean duly earned his first yellow card in a yellow shirt for that bit of silliness, some 14 minutes from time.

Inevitably, Dutchman Leandro Bacuna, whose surging run had been ended by Medel 25 yards out from goal, compounded the dismay by striking home the resultant free-kick with much style, the flight of the ball looping up and over ... or was it around ... the defensive wall, leaving Marshall glued to the spot. Villa's first goal for 7½ hours. Much glee from the enormous Holte End behind that goal – Villa's 12th man, if we are to believe their banner.

This was all quite harsh on us to be honest, as, while not really offering much of a goal threat (again!), City had put up a reasonably stubborn, yet composed performance.

Sadly, a second, slightly scruffy headed goal, 6 minutes from time, from Libor Kozak, ended things as a contest. Not for the first time this season in my opinion, City seemed to lose shape somewhat once they were facing defeat (see Chelsea away) and the final moments saw more Villa pressure, with Jordan Bowery shooting into the side netting. Only a few unproductive corners and an uninspiring Whitts free-kick were offered in response. 'Don't Sack Mackay, You're Going to Have a Riot on Your Hands,' sang the City faithful.

Malky was fairly philosophical in defeat though, commenting, 'I'm not too disappointed because if we show that kind of application we'll be fine. Ultimately it was a good goal that made the difference.'

Ah well, 'In Malky We Trust', eh?

Dear Diary,

Sunday, 10 November 2013

I wouldn't normally do this, but I followed today's results via Radio 5 Live.

I don't enjoy 5 Live. It is very England biased and PL dominated. Though these days, it can provide an objective way of keeping up with the games of our rivals. Sunderland won against Man. City, somehow. Newcastle did Spurs. Wales lost at rugby (League).

Man. U. v. Arsenal was the main game on 5 Live. United won 1-0 thanks to RVP, though the commentary was more concerned with the antics of Jack Wilshere than anything else. Engerland see ...?

Respect to Ian Wright for calling Ramsay 'Rambo', mind. *('Respect???' Is this your DJ mate, Giggsy, writing this bit, Dave?)*

'Rambo?' said the female presenter.

'Yes' said Wrightey.

Why do they let women present football, eh? I mean, why do they do that??

The Man. U. game had been interrupted by reports from the Jacks game. Stoke went 2-0 ahead (cue cheers in the hairdresser's car) but the JBs soon turned it round to win 3-2. Damn.

But in stoppage time, Stoke (a team I have learned to despise over the years) smash home a penalty from Charlie Austin, and the Jacks enjoy a second successive dreary Sunday. A chorus of Delilah breaks out somewhere in Pontprennau.

It's fun keeping a diary, isn't it?

Dear Diary,
Monday, 11 November 2013

Joe Mason has gone on loan to Bolton. Is this a great opportunity for a youngster to gain first team action, or confirmation that Joe doesn't feature in Malky's plans?

I fear the latter.

Dear Diary,
Wednesday, 13 November 2013

As you were, soldier!!

Turns out that Joe Mason has been recalled from his loan spell. Odemwingie and/or Gestede seem to have acquired knocks and Malky now needs Joe for cover. So, after one training session at Bolton – he is back to being a Bluebird.

Or did Tan loan him out and Malky bring him back? Conspiracy theories begin here.

Dave, did you know that, on this day in 1965, John Toshack made his debut for Cardiff City, aged merely 16 years and 23 days?

Amazingly, no Gareth, though I know he was the youngest player to appear for us until Aaron Ramsay broke the record in 2007.

Dear Diary,
Friday, 15 November 2013

A real treat for us on the Cardiff City Phone-in tonight. Special guest in the studio, Derek Brazil. *(Brazily!)* Derek was in to help plug the 1993 Promotion Celebration taking place next week. What a star he was, as he regaled us with stories from that season, memories of Dai Hunt (honest!) and what it's like to play for both Cardiff City and Swansea (he played twelve games on loan at The Vetch in 1991). We also learned that Jason Perry was as nice a guy off the pitch as he was volatile on it, that Tony Bird once indulged in an impromptu jet skiing session in Donegal to the amazement of his fellow players, and that Phil Stant used to live in a caravan opposite Sully Island. Derek wasn't able to explain why.

Dear Diary,

Saturday, 16 November 2013

Joe Ledley today earned his 50th international cap for Wales in a 1–1 draw against Finland at the Cardiff City Stadium.

Other highlights of the game included ... errrm ... errrmmm ...

Dear Diary,

Monday, 18 November 2013

On the other hand though ...

We read via Wales Online today, that City defender Declan John has led Wales to a 6-goal win and qualification to the UEFA Under-19 Championships elite round.

Wales went into the match against Moldova needing a 7 (yes, 7!) goal swing to overhaul Holland, assuming the Dutch did not win or draw their final game against Georgia. Chike Kandi grabbed the 'all important' (hate that phrase) 6th goal in the last minute to pip the Dutch for a place in the elite round, though exactly what the 'elite round' comprises remains a mystery to me. Five City players appeared in the starting line-up with three of them scoring. The Under-17s have also qualified for the elite round in their tournament and, despite some woeful results earlier in the group, the Under-21s are in second place.

The City scorers were John himself, with a penalty, Tommy O'Sullivan and Abdi Noor.

Of course, these guys will all be household names by the time you read this.

Dear Diary,

Tuesday, 19 November 2013

Funny how a diary goes, innit?

In a discussion with Gareth about which club has the best youth policy today, there was general consensus that Southampton may lay credible claim to that crown. Look at the current England squad, for example.

Then we discover that Cardiff City beat their Under-10 team 9–2.

9–2?

Under-10???

Shit, I have shirts older than that.

Dear Diary,

Wednesday, 20 November 2013

Cardiff City FC seem to be going all 'give-us-your-feedback' these days, like some cash-starved local authority.

The club's official website today even invited fans to send their 'Dear Santa' wishes to the club. I swear to you that they actually did this. Fans could submit their Xmas wishes direct to the club's website.

I mean, what were they thinking, what did they expect? Here is the letter I sent. Be careful what you wish for Mr Tan:

Dear Santa,

Please can you bring back our famous blue shirts and Bluebird badge. That would make my Xmas dreams come true. All I want for Christmas, is Blue.

David Collins, Pontprennau, Cardiff.

I will keep you posted on whether this happens on Christmas morn.

Dear Diary,

Thursday, 22 November 2013

Ah, some days, are just made for living.

One of the most underrated defenders in the history of Welsh football, pictured here alongside Jason Perry.

The Cardiff City Supporters' Trust 1993 Promotion Party tonight was a right hoot. I won't dwell on the fact that I had a photo taken with Nathan Blake, and another with Jason Perry, but shall cut to the highlights:

Paul Millar:	'Neil Matthews' flat was a den of iniquity.'
Carl Dale:	'I dunno, what is a legend??'
Paul Ramsey:	'Blakey could play anywhere.'
Nathan Blake:	'I hated playing centre-half.'
Damon Searle:	'Don't tell 'em about Jacksons.'
Fan from the audience:	'Why did Paul Ramsey tell me to f**k off at Scunthorpe?'

Dear Diary,

Friday, 22 November 2013

Now I know what you're thinking.

We are playing Man. U. in two days' time, and he hasn't even mentioned it.

Well, we covered it on the phone-in tonight, and I think I sense a feeling that 'anything other than a 3-0 defeat is a bonus'. I can see where they are coming from. I don't think our season will be defined by a game against Man. U. But this is the bright lights for sure. We is living 'La Vida Loca'. I just hope they take it easy with us.

So what do we think? Will they score 2 quick goals and murder us? Or will we keep it tight and bundle in a corner in the 88th minute? Will Giggs do the Ayatollah? Will Rooney???

I reckon it will be 4–4.

Dear Diary,

Saturday, 23 November 2013

My son Dan works in a coffee shop in St David's 2. City players seem to pop in for their mocca-boco-choca-shocka at regular intervals. Look at this text dialogue frrinstance:

DAN: 'Just served Cornelius, he bought a banana and bottle of water.'
DAD: 'Is he ready for tomorrow??'
DAN: 'Looks it, he's huge!! About 7ft.'

What could possibly go wrong, eh?

Dear Diary,

Sunday, 24 November 2013

Cardiff City 2 – 2 Man. Utd

k/o 4.00 p.m.

When you fantasise about your team being in the Premier League, this is the kind of fixture you have in your mind. Let's face it, City fans had a long time to fantasise – fifty-one years – so we had time to get the fantasy just right. The problem is, in my fantasy we were playing at a different ground – dear departed Ninian Park – and they were playing in red and we were playing in blue. Hmm ... enough of the fantasy.

We hadn't played United in any competition since 1974/75, when they had their one-season interlude in the old Second Division. The Ninian Park clash that year has since entered the realms of folklore, with tales of United 'bovver boys' (complete with Doc Marten boots and scarves on both wrists) rampaging down Tudor Street as they 'ran' the locals. So it's been a fair old wait to play the buggers again. (I was at that game!)

City put up a decent show in this game. We needed a late equaliser to grab a point, but in truth we gave as good as we got here. We knocked the ball around, enjoyed a large share of possession and territory, and did not look out of place in this company.

One of the main talking points afterwards was the non-sending off of Wayne Rooney, after he deliberately kicked Jordon Mutch. While a red card was certainly warranted, to be fair City should, by the same token, have had Gary Medel dismissed for shoving Fellaini in the face while they tussled prior to a set piece.

Incidentally, Fellaini – and the bird's nest he keeps on his head – are getting very familiar with the new stadium. He has played there three times this season, for Everton, Belgium and now United. Good quiz question, that.

United took the lead after 15 minutes, when Turner played a loose pass just outside the City penalty area. Valencia switched the play, and the move ended with Rooney's shot deflecting in off Medel, the deflection meaning that even Marshall had no chance of saving it.

City were not daunted by this, and continued to 'play'. They equalised just after the 30-minute mark with the best move of the game. Whitts threaded a nice ball through to Mutch, who had found some space in the 'hole' between their back four and midfield. Even better than Mutch's movement was his pass behind the defence for Campbell to run on to – and Campbell showed great composure to knock the shot past De Gea.

It looked like it was going to be level at half-time, but alas, it was not to be. Rooney took a corner, something went wrong with the marking, and Evra scored – not the first time this season he has done that, Malky mate ...

After the break, City continued to compete, and Mr Mackay made an enterprising substitution by bringing on Craig Noone for his first taste of Premier League action. Malky kept putting

Noone on the bench, and I was beginning to wonder when he was ever going to bring him on – but here, he did.

Noone made a decent impact, trying to beat men and carry the ball forward. At the death, he was fouled, and from the free-kick, Whitts knocked it in and Kim got in between United defenders (who probably decided he wasn't worth marking!) to nod the ball in. A deserved draw. City are doing okay.

Dear Diary,
Monday, 25 November 2013

Do you know, back in the late 1980s when Gareth and I first started scribbling down fanzine articles, the only way to keep up with events at Ninian Park was via the back pages of the local paper on Friday teatimes. Many a time I dashed home from work to read about games against Newport or Bournemouth. These days, though, football is everywhere. Global superstars are beamed live to our homes via a series of digital contraptions.

Today, for example, we read via the BBC Ceefax pages that Wayne Rooney has 'tweeted' about a foul that I just watched on *Match of the Day 2*, via iPlayer.

Blimey, at this rate we'll be able to go an entire season without leaving the house.

I watched Rooney's foul over and over again this evening (you can't watch *MOTD2* on iPlayer until gone midnight, actually – so technically this should be tomorrow's entry perhaps). I just hope someone plants him in the World Cup next year and only collects a yellow card. Mind you, I had to chuckle at Gary Medel throwing a left-hook up at Fellaini in the dying moments yesterday. Can't wait for the rematch if they meet up in South America next June. Medel will murder him.

Dear Diary,
Tuesday, 26 November 2013

Life's never dull, is it?

'Rudy completes a Blackburn switch,' announced the club website today. The Cardiff City striker (that is the website's description, not ours by the way) has joined Blackburn Rovers on loan with a view to a permanent move in January.

Clearly the banana bought by Cornelius last week was just the tonic he needed to bring him back to fitness, as the abundance of forward talent we now have available means we can even loan out Rudy.

Unless he does a Joe Mason on us.

Dear Diary,
Wednesday, 27 November 2013

This is getting ridiculous. How is a guy meant to keep up with all this?

Joe Mason's loan deal to Bolton is now back on! He has apparently completed an 'emergency' loan move and joined Bolton Wanderers after all. The loan spell ends on 5 January 2014. I just know we will draw Bolton in the FA Cup at this rate.

Dear Diary,
Thursday, 28 November 2013

Hey, what's this? Another new City website – www.theninian.com. 'Football from the Cardiff City perspective' apparently. Might be worth a look …

Wow. It's like Star-Trek-does-Football-Focus. This eye-popping site features such graphics as a pie chart showing 'average defensive actions' to support their claim that Steve Caulker should play for England, along with the news that he was successful in 45 per cent of his headed duels and a whopping 79 per cent of his tackles.

Blimey, and I thought me and Gareth were geeks …

Dear Diary,
Friday, 29 November 2013

I have decided to take a few days away this weekend. A boozy few days away.

Movember Bluebirds!

But fear not, thanks to the wonders of modern technology I discover via www.walesonline.co.uk that City Chairman Mehmet Dalman has dismissed claims from controversial Turkish manager Yilmaz Vural that he is set to join Cardiff City. Apparently this guy is also linked with Pompey and Sheffield United. He has managed all the teams in Turkey except Galatasaray, Fenerbahce and Besiktas, apparently. So that would mean that that he has managed ... uhm ... uhm ...

Dear Diary,

Saturday, 30 November 2013

Cardiff City 0 – 3 Arsenal

k/o 3.00 p.m.

The scoreline looked bad here – and certainly didn't do our goal difference any good – but City were not outclassed by 'the Arse'. With less than 10 minutes to go, we were only a goal down, and had an outside chance of getting something out of the game.

The League leaders began ominously when, from virtually the first move of the game, Wilshere – whom I have not previously rated much as an attacking player – hit a thunderbolt of a shot which crashed against Marshall's post.

The game then settled down, and City had a half-chance with a glancing header from Campbell, which keeper Szczesny clearly knew was going wide, as he did not even react to it. Then, after a quarter of an hour – the same kind of time when Man. Utd took the lead against us – the 'old boy returning' curse struck, and Aaron Ramsey gave the visitors the lead. There didn't look to be too much danger when Ozil crossed from City's right, as Arsenal did not have many men in the box. But one of them was Rambo, and he has now apparently added towering headers to his many attacking attributes. There the ball lay in the back of the net before anybody had time to blink.

Ramsey declined to celebrate, but should the bugger have scored against us at all? After all, Bellamy came on against us in the Carling Cup final for Liverpool, and clearly wasn't even trying ...

City were still 'in it' until near the end, but our only real chance came from another Campbell header early in the second half. This time Szczesny had to make the save, and he managed to pull off an exceptional one.

In the last few minutes, Flamini ended a flowing move by knocking the ball in for Arsenal's 2nd, to kill off the game. Then Ramsey scored another. The boy from Caerphilly done good, and got a good reception. He was even applauded for his goals. Wenger commented afterwards that the City supporters deserved a Man of the Match award for themselves, which was a nice remark. But then it's easy to be nice when you've just won 3–0.

PS. I've got a thing about players who should only play for the team it sounds like they should play for. So Derek Brazil should only play for Brazil, Mike England for England, Matt Derbyshire for either Derby or Chesterfield – d'ya see what I mean? So why isn't Wilshere playing for Swindon Town? (Maybe Justin Edinburgh should be manager of Hearts or Hibs. Let's move on ...)

Five

IN THE BLEAK MIDWINTER

Dear Diary,

Sunday, 1 December 2013

Fun with text:
Our mate Richard: 'Dave Jones sacked.'
Me: 'Yes. Just heard. Malky to Fulham, DJ here?'
Richard: *(silence ...)*

Dear Diary,

Monday, 2 December 2013

Mehmet now denies the Turk's claims that they ever met. He seems to be making quite an effort to put this story down, doesn't he?

Dear Diary,

Tuesday, 3 December 2013

'City sign current Welsh International!'

Well, technically true – Declan John has signed a new contract. We will take it.

Anyway. At last, midweek football is back. After seemingly having played only once or twice in November, we now face three games in eight days.

'Stoke away on a Wednesday night, Gareth? Do you fancy it?'
  'Dave, I think the words "Stoke" and "Wednesday night" might give you a clue there.'
  We decide to listen to it on the wireless.

Dear Diary,

Wednesday, 4 December 2013

Stoke City 0 – 0 Cardiff City

k/o 7.45 p.m.

Dear Diary,

Friday, 6 December 2013

Ah, the *South Wales Echo*. Old School news reporting in this age of Twitter, iPads and interactive message boards. Proper news on the back page of a newspaper. Still lifts the soul, doesn't it? Even for Crystal Palace away.

  'I will do the Ayatollah for City fans,' says Danny Gabbidon.

  I am supposed to be seeing him next week in Cwmbran. I wonder if he will do it there?

Dear Diary,

Saturday, 7 December 2013

Crystal Palace 2 – 0 Cardiff City

k/o 3.00 p.m.

Thanks to an intricate exchange of texts, Gareth and I manage to rendezvous at the 'Boro' (aka the Borough Arms in

St Mary Street) for this one, but need to act fast as they are not showing the game.

We skip across to Charlie Brown's *(skip???)* only to meet similar despair. Finally, we arrive at the Queens Vaults, just where yellow-shirted Cardiff City can be seen live from South London, via some Albanian TV channel. Marvellous.

Whether all this was actually worthwhile is open to debate, as Gareth explains so objectively and eloquently below:

City were shite in this game.

In the opening minute, Whitts and Mutch worked an opening on the right side of the Palace penalty area, Whitts whipped in a cross and Fraizer Campbell sneaked in between the central defenders for a free header. He kept it low, he headed it back the way it had come – all the textbook stuff. But Julian Speroni is a decent goalie, and he managed to jerk himself back into position and make a reflex save. In the Championship, that might have been a goal. In the Premier League, usually not.

Alas for City, that proved to be our first, last and only chance of the game. Palace took control and dominated the rest of it. This was despite Palace having two men up front (Chamakh and Jerome), and therefore only four in midfield, up against City's usual five-man midfield. But the 'extra man' we theoretically had in that area did not in any way trouble Palace. So is this five-man midfield thing working? No, it is not. Will Malky change it? I don't think so.

The first goal we actually missed. After about 5 minutes of play, the 'stream' in the pub shut off for a bit, and when it came back on, City were 1-0 down. 'Bet you Jerome scored,' I muttered. We gave Cameron Jerome his League debut nine years ago, back in the Lennie Lawrence era. Eventually we saw the action replay – and yes, it was Jerome who scored, bundling in a header from close range. Who was at fault for this one? God knows ...

Another ex-City player turning out for the Eagles is Danny Gabbidon. He was one of our stars when we were back in the third tier, not long after the turn of the millennium. Strange to see him still turning out in the Premier League. Last season it seemed as if City were probably too good for his level now. It would be 'funny' (funny peculiar, not funny ha-ha) if Palace now stayed up, and City went down ...

The second goal came midway through the second half. A deep cross came in from Jason Puncheon on the Palace left, Caulker managed to head it out running towards his own goal, but it fell to Chamakh, who was unmarked in our area. He chested it down and hit a controlled half-volley into the unguarded corner of the net.

The fly in the ointment here was Medel. He saw Chamakh unmarked at the beginning of the move, and didn't track him, even though he was the nearest City player to him. So Chamakh had all the time in the world when the ball fell at his feet. Well done, Medel!

I am getting increasingly irked by the £11 million Spaniard. (Chilean!) *He is uncomfortable in possession near our penalty area and is dispossessed in this 'danger area' nearly every game (it happened again in this one) – and he does not always track back. Whatever his positive qualities might be, as a defensive midfielder he is rubbish. Will Malky drop him, or delegate his defensive role to somebody else? I don't think so, because Medel seems immune to criticism. If Malky drops him, it is an admission that he has wasted all that money in signing him. I think Medel will stay in the team, and will cost us more goals.*

After this game, I am also convinced that City are going down. Malky might keep reshuffling his pack, but if you have a bad pack, in the end it doesn't matter. We are the last game on Match of the Day, *we haven't won any of the last five games, and we haven't scored in the last three. We are 2 points away from the bottom three, and at this rate, we will soon be in it. Situation (now I have accepted it rationally) 'hopeless but not desperate'.*

Positives? Declan John played again at left-back (for the injured Andrew Taylor), and the teenager from the Valleys again looked not out of place in the Premier. Perhaps he will keep his place when Taylor is fit again, as he looks to have more penetration going forward. Andreas Cornelius, our big blond Danish striker, who has been missing injured since the start of the season, came on as a sub for the last 25 minutes, and had a couple of decent touches.

And as for Malky? Well, he sticks to the same forma-tion (4-5-1), which is increasingly looking like a ball and chain around City's ankle. His post-match comments seem increasingly deluded – he said here that, had Campbell scored, everything could have been different. No reference to the fact that we did not create another chance for the remaining 89 minutes. No reference to the fact that Palace outplayed us.

To stay up, we have to finish above three sides and Palace were one of the 'certainties' to finish below us. But they look better than us now ...

The fans have taken to singing 'if you sack Mackay', to the tune of 'Achy Breaky Heart'. The bad thing is, we need to make some effective loan signings in the transfer window to stay up. We need to drop Medel (or change his role). We need to change our formation. All of these things are more likely to happen with a different manager. We might now be getting to the stage where we are better off if we do sack Mackay.

One of the guys who has been available since the start of the season is Tony Pulis – but because we have stayed loyal to Mackay, we can't have him now, because he has gone to Palace .... I know this sounds disloyal to Malky, who is a good guy, but I am just trying to be brutally objective about the grim business of staying in the Premier League – a league where Malky has never managed. If he is going to learn how to do it, he needs to start doing it quickly.

An interesting point about this game is that it was covered in the Sunday Times *by Brian Glanville. The doyen of football writers, now aged 83, he was writing for the same paper when City were last in the top flight, fifty-one years ago.*

Dear Diary,

Sunday, 8 December 2013

Funny how times change, isn't it?

Ten years ago, today would have been eagerly awaited amongst all City fans. The third round FA Cup draw. Always exciting. We'd have been sat in front of the telly, dreaming of a plum home draw with Leeds or Liverpool. Twenty years ago it would have been the radio on a Monday lunchtime. Now that was romance, I can tell you.

These days, though, a visit from Leeds holds less glamour, while we play the likes of Liverpool on a weekly basis now, of course.

I fancy an away trip to a ground we haven't been to. Like Fleetwood or Crawley Town. Even Shrewsbury's new ground would do. That ain't far is it?

Yeah, or Stevenage. That would be ideal.

First out ... Barnsley. *(Bin there ...)*

Liverpool pull Oldham. They will be happy. Stevenage and Palace both come out of the hat before us. Then, we get ... Newcastle away. They will murder us and it's miles away. It will be freezing in January too.

We decide to go.

Dear Diary,
Monday, 9 December 2013

Funny how a theme sometimes emerges over these pages, eh? 'Players not celebrating goals.' Discuss. Following Rambo's gentlemanly display at CCS recently, along with Jerome's reasonably muted glee on Saturday (not sure about that thumb sucking thing he does though) we see that in tonight's Monday night fixture *(?????)*, former Swansea striker, Danny Graham, acted with equal restraint when giving the Tigers an early lead over the Jacks down west. That was Graham's first goal since leaving Swansea over a year ago. And to think we tried to sign him.

Come to think of it, 1 goal in thirty-odd games would probably secure him a place in our side at the moment.

Dear Diary,
Tuesday, 10 December 2013

Match-fixing allegations fill the tabloids in this season of 'Good Cheer'.

Blackburn striker DJ Campbell has denied all allegations, though. He is 100 per cent innocent and looking forward to playing in the 1–1 draw against Millwall on Saturday.

Dear Diary,

Wednesday, 10 December 2013

So where do you stand on Pyro Technics at games then, Gareth?
  Pyro Technics? Is he that new midfielder we are chasing from Colombia?
  Yes, Gareth, he is the Colombian.

Dear Diary,

Thursday, 12 December 2013

Interesting sequence of events presented to us by this evening's fixtures. I popped into my local on the way home from work to catch Spurs' Europa League tie against Anji, which was being shown live on ITV4.

During the second half, the Tottenham youngster, Ryan Fredericks, glided his way into the box. On feeling the brush of the defender's leg, the lad inevitably flung himself to the ground as if brought down by a sniper's bullet. He then threw his arms up in horror as the ref waved away his protest, only to rejoice when the (and I quote) '6th official' gave the penalty, which was coolly slotted away by Spanish striker Roberto Soldado.

Europa League? ITV 4? 6th official? Football on Thursdays???
Sometimes I struggle to recognise football at all these days.

Dear Diary,

Friday, 13 December 2013

Thanks to last week's Selhurst Shambles, we now commence a series of 'must win' games against the lesser lights of the PL. Half-time in that fixture had seen Gareth and I rehearse our usual debate as to whether Mackay should keep things tight and poach a late equaliser, or step up the pace earlier. Odemwingie came on as City went 4-4-2, which meant Gareth shaded that debate. Again. Though the nomadic Nigerian driver is rapidly emerging as a front runner for my 'Just What Does This Player Actually Do?' Award.

Perhaps I will find out tomorrow, for I have managed to secure a ticket for the Baggies fixture. 'West Bromwich Albion', a proper team with a proper name – Hull City owner, please note.

Proper kit too. Cardiff City Chairman, please take note.

Dear Diary,

Saturday, 14 December 2013

Cardiff City 1 – 0 West Bromwich Albion

k/o 3.00 p.m.

I said before this game that if City were 2 goals down with 20 minutes to go, and didn't go 4-4-2, then Malky would deserve the sack. In the event, we didn't have to worry, because he went with 4-4-2 from the start – for the first time this season.

The formation actually worked, because City dominated the game. Whether Odemwingie and Campbell were the best combination to play together remains in doubt. I thought they would play well together, but they rarely linked up, and perhaps neither is physically strong enough – perhaps they need a strong man to play up front with either one or the other of them. But oddly, although this seemed increasingly apparent, Cornelius made no appearance – instead Maynard, another lightweight, came on for the last 10 minutes, having come on for Campbell. So we paid £8 million for this Scandinavian geezer and now Malky won't even put him on the pitch. Odd, very odd.

Okay, enough of the formation, on with the game. City began well and had the Baggies under pressure for most of the first half, but were unable to score. Increasingly, fears of a breakaway goal and another defeat abounded, but no, midway through the second period, Noone (starting a Premier League game for the first time) put in a cross from the right. Whittingham, who had done little of note up to that point, had come in from his wing; he rose majestically above a defender and placed a superbly timed header into the corner of the net. Is this the first time Whittingham has ever headed a ball? Probably! He should do it more often. (Maybe he is learning from Ramsey.)

West Brom., who were fairly poor throughout, managed to mount a rearguard action towards the end, but City held on. Marshall made one superb reflex stop, but apart from that, City were largely untroubled.

City positives: Craig Noone came in for his first start of the season on the right, and made more of an attacking impact than Don Cowie had managed during his run in the side. Noone actually crossed a ball on his right foot, plus he won a tackle, both firsts for the player in a City shirt. He put crosses into the area on several occasions, and finally this produced City's winner.

Another positive was the formation – despite being outnumbered in midfield, City dominated, as we had ourselves been dominated at Palace a week earlier, despite outnumbering them. So maybe Malky is learning. City also played it out from the back better than we did at the start of the season – we are gradually improving in this department.

Negatives: Odemwingie, against his old club, did a lot of showboating, but there is often no end product. His combination with Fraizer Campbell did not look particularly effective. Kevin Theo surges forward into space, and goes as far up the pitch as he can. In comparison, Andrew Taylor, back at left-back, seems only able to advance a certain distance up the pitch before he gets a 'nosebleed', turns around and passes the ball backwards. I feel Declan John is better, and should have kept his place.

An hour after this game, Albion sacked their manager, Steve Clarke. Cardiff City Stadium – graveyard of Premier League managers!

Dear Diary,
Sunday, 15 December 2013

Spent most of today in my new Xmas jumper, reliving the glories of yesterday. Despite the cold and rain, all were in agreement that was almost a season-saving victory, even in December. Though, how the *Wales On Sunday* could give so many players decent marks was beyond me.

Now I know that my seat near an exit meant that I must have missed a third of the game thanks to late arrivals, early half-time piss takers and fidgeting kids, but really – Odemwingie, 7?

Taylor, 8? Jordon Mutch our 'most consistent player so far this season'? Really??? I'd have thought one D. Marshall Esq. may lay claim to that crown.

Talking of honours and accolades, it's the time of the year when the BBC hands out its annual Sports Personality of the Year Awards, isn't it? BBC Wales somehow gave the Welsh rugby team 'Team of the Year' – clearly a defeat to Japan carries more weight than a League Championship – while Leigh Halfpenny has somehow been nominated for tonight's 'BBC Sports Personality of the Year'. Weren't his best results achieved on the Lions tour, though? That wasn't even shown on BBC, was it? Strange logic by the Beeb.

Dear Diary,
Monday, 16 December 2013

Well that went well, didn't it? Any feel good factor or air of stability which had settled over us after that WBA victory lasted little over twenty-four hours, thanks to the latest outburst from our 'colourful' owner.

The morning media had raised our hopes with the news that Malky was targeting three new signings in the January transfer window (do we really need more defenders?), only for Tan to declare that he won't be given 'a single penny' in January.

In a sensational statement, released by chief executive Simon Lim, the club accused Mackay of overspending by £15 million during the summer – a move, Lim officially revealed, that led directly to the removal of Mackay's close aide and former head of recruitment, Iain Moody.

Mackay's future was again plunged into grave doubt, with Lim and Tan publicly slamming the boss for 'unfairly raising supporters' expectations' after the Scot revealed he was targeting three new signings in the January transfer window.

Tan was extremely upset to read quotes from the manager concerning the possibility of new recruits, before he had been informed whether funds would be made available. He believed that doing so unfairly raises supporter expectations, placing unnecessary pressure on the club.

This seems to take things to a new low, doesn't it? Clear evidence of the disharmony at the club. Was Malky simply thinking aloud – just reading out his letter to Santa? Or do Tan and Lim have a point by telling him that he has enough toys already, and that he doesn't even play with the ones he has.

As ever, the truth probably lies somewhere between the two, but as evidence of the chasm between the two, it's about as good an example as you could find.

Dear Diary,

Tuesday, 17 December 2013

Gianfranco Zola booked into a hotel in Cardiff next week apparently. Worth a flutter?

Dear Diary,

Wednesday, 18 December 2013

Tim Hartley, chair of Cardiff City Supporters' Trust (never one to shirk an issue), writes today:

> We are very disappointed at the tone of statement from the club and we fear this will further strain the relationship between Malky Mackay and Mr Tan.
>
> It is normal practice for any club manager to draw up a wish list before the January transfer window.
>
> While the Bluebirds have made a steady start to their first season in the Premier League, it is important to strengthen in January as all our rivals no doubt will be. Malky Mackay was stating publicly the views of many fans about the need to bolster the team to give the club the best chance of remaining in the Premier League. Teams including West Ham United, Sunderland, Hull and Crystal Palace are all looking to strengthen next month.
>
> While Mr Tan has backed the club financially, so have fans. They have bought up every single season ticket available despite the undoubted disquiet and anger over the imposed rebrand and changes to the club's identity.

We don't want to see anything which undermines the manager and affects the team following the excellent win over West Bromwich Albion.

Mr Hartley added: 'We are unaware of whether or not there was overspending on players this summer but fans remain behind Malky Mackay.'

Dear Diary,

Thursday, 19 December 2013

'Resign or be sacked,' says Tan.
   'I am appalled,' says Brendan Rodgers.
   'Can I have £2 on Zola?' says diarist to bookie.

Dear Diary,

Friday, 20 December 2013

6 o'clock already, I was just in the middle of a dream ...

But instead of being awoken by Susanna Hoffs from the Bangles (now there's a thought), it was the somewhat more industrial tones of Vince Alm that disturbed my slumber. Vince (from Cardiff City Supporters' Club) was up early today and speaking much sense on Radio Wales about how we should all be celebrating these heady days in the top flight, yet instead we are worried by these amazing distractions arising from Tan's 'resign or be sacked' ultimatum.

Vince spoke like a man weary of the world. He tried so hard to be fair, explaining how we have to remember that Tan had put a lot of money into the club. 'It's sad really. If you look at everything else, he is ticking all the boxes, doing a fantastic job expanding the stadium, a new training ground, putting money into the community.' Poor Vince. I feel his pain.

Yilmaz Vural is still being tipped as Cardiff's next manager.

In other rumours ... Dave Jones set to return, 'household name' waiting in the wings, Malky to claim unfair dismissal. By lunchtime, one 'resign or be sacked' message board thread had over 8,000 views. Blimey, I have been to games with smaller crowds than that.

Mad innit? 3,000 of us are off to one of the great cathedrals of the English game tomorrow yet, not for the first time this season, off the field shenanigans are dominating this diary. My first text today arrived at 7.20 a.m., from a despairing fellow sufferer. Radio Wales devoted an entire hour to the fracas on their morning call slot and the national press have also caught up with this story big time, as we sink lower and lower down the ladder of respectability towards becoming the laughing stock of the year.

No wonder they call today 'Black Friday'.

Dear Diary,

Saturday, 21 December 2013

Liverpool 3 – 1 Cardiff City

k/o 12.25 p.m.

Thanks to some fancy footwork and a few called-in favours, we actually managed to get tickets for this one. I will gloss over Collins' appalling driving skills and sense of direction, but he managed to get us to Anfield in time for this lunchtime kick-off. Somehow.

City's preparations for this game were hampered by Vincent Tan's calls for Malky to resign his post. Not the ideal run-up to a match against one of the division's in-form teams, who would go top if they beat us!

City looked pretty good during the opening 20 minutes. Odemwingie and Noone, working together, sometimes harried their defenders into giving the ball away. But on one of these occasions, the ball came to Mutch, whose low cross-shot drifted harmlessly across the area – which had no City player in it. This is the problem of playing 4-5-1, and having Odemwingie come across to hassle defenders – if we get the ball, there is nobody in the box for us. But it is good to see that Noone and Odemwingie are perhaps learning to play 'the Malky way'.

Noone was looking particularly threatening. On one occasion, he beat left-back Flanagan (part of Liverpool's duo of Flanagan and Allen – am I the only one who has noticed this combination?) and crossed with his right. On another, he cut inside and fired in a shot with his favoured left, which Mignolet palmed over the bar.

There were danger signs for City down our left, though, where Taylor was being threatened by both wide man Raheem Sterling and right-back Glen Johnson, both of whom could beat him for pace with ease. Nobody seemed to be going over there to help him out. Whittingham seemed to be too far forward, and Medel, who was covering that side of the pitch, looked uninterested in getting involved.

We started to be bothered by Luis Suarez. By half-time, Suarez's constant movement had destroyed us, and given Liverpool a 3–0 lead. It wasn't just Suarez's movement, though; we couldn't cope with Jordan Henderson's movement, either.

After 17 minutes, Henderson ran through off the ball, and Medel, despite seeing him go past him, did not react. The ball did not come to Henderson, and the move petered out – but if it had done, he would have been clear on goal. Eight minutes later, Suarez quickly darted infield, off the ball, and again, Medel, despite being the closest City player to him, made no effort to track the run. The ball came back to Suarez, and although he steered a great volley into the corner of the net, he was under no pressure at all.

We had a penalty shout when Caulker was clearly held by Skrtel, but this was not given – neither did we get one when this move was repeated several times during the course of the game. However, despite this chance City were, in truth, now being overrun by Liverpool, only Marshall's saves keeping us in the game.

It was finished as a contest in the last 5 minutes of the half, when Liverpool scored another 2 goals. First, from our own free-kick, we packed the box – such is our wont – and left only Theo and Taylor standing on the halfway line. Nobody was guarding the 'hole' midway between their area and halfway, where Medel or Gunnarsson should have been posted.

The result was Theo being forced forward to head the ball back in; the ball fell to Liverpool, who quickly fed Suarez.

With Theo now out of position, Liverpool had three against one – and our one was Taylor, who is not the quickest. Suarez fed Sterling, who knocked the ball into our empty net with ridiculous ease. The 3rd goal saw us beaten again by Suarez's movement; it ended with his curling a shot around Marshall and into the far corner.

Hurry up, Dave. I am starving.

Ah, that's better.

Medel appeared at this point to be having no impact on the game at all. At one point, Joe Allen – hardly known as a dribbler – went past him as though he wasn't there. Now, Gunnarsson and Whittingham were having precious little effect either – but then, neither of them cost us £11 million. All Medel seemed to be doing was pointing – he never seemed to try and mark anybody himself. I have always been suspicious of players who point all the time.

After the break, City enjoyed long periods of possession. The goal came after 57 minutes, when, from the inevitable free-kick, Mutch was left completely unmarked at the back post. Turner cleverly left the ball but blocked the Liverpool defender, and Mutch guided his header into the far corner. Mutch had another chance which he headed over, and – despite the possession and territory – that was that for City.

It was a nice day out for the City fans, though, despite the defeat. They kept up a constant wall of sound in support of Malky, with numbers such as 'Don't Sack Mackay' (by now an established favourite), 'Go Back to Malaysia' (to the tune of '1–0 to the Arsenal') and also '4–3, We're Gonna Win 4–3'. The last two were more ironic than hopeful – maybe the first was too ...

Dear Diary,

Sunday, 22 December 2013

Gareth, Tan has done a U-turn! Seems that he has announced today that Malky will remain manager for the 'foreseeable future'. Chairman Mehmet Dalman has created what he calls a 'window of dialogue'.

What will we have to protest against now though, Dave?
Oh, we'll think of something ...

Dear Diary,

Thursday, 26 December 2013

Cardiff City 0 – 3 Southampton

k/o 3.00 p.m.

This was an abject performance by City, who gave the game up in the first half hour. There is not a lot to say about the game, other than that. I started making notes, and after 15 minutes, I didn't bother anymore.

Southampton had clearly watched the Liverpool game, and noted our weakness down the left, where Whitts and Taylor make a dangerously slow combination. Now, Saints don't really have a quick right-winger (they have Schneiderlin, who is quite slow), but nevertheless they blasted down that side, twice, and then switched the play quickly over to the left, where twice Jay Rodriguez ghosted into the far-post area, unseen and unmarked, and twice knocked the ball into the net. After 27 minutes, Rickie Lambert added a 3rd, and that was that. Game over.

Now, back in the old days when we used to regularly play Halifax Town and Rochdale, me and my mate Paul had a 'three goal rule'. This meant that, if City went 3 down at home, we had to leave Ninian Park ASAP and retire to the pub. In the Premier League, this ruling apparently no longer applies, and I had to stay and watch the rest of a dull game.

The only other thing I can add is this. Before the game, we debated what our starting line-ups should be. By the end, after three substitutions, Malky had all eleven of Paul's starting line-up, and ten of mine. So we seem to be doing a better job of picking the side than Malky ...

Okay, we all know Malky has been badly treated by Vincent Tan – if he wanted him out, he should have paid him off and sacked him, not left him to dangle like this. But there may be a rational case for parting company with Malky – as I wrote after the Palace defeat, three games ago. The fans all chanted 'Don't Sack Mackay', as we lost 3-0 at home to Southampton. So what constitutes a bad enough result, and performance, to consider getting rid of the manager?

Dear Diary,
Friday, 27 December 2013

'Don't sack Mackay, Malky Mac ...'

So we now understand the true definition of the phrase 'foreseeable future'. It seems as though the term defines a period lasting approximately 27 minutes. For once the unmarked Ricky Lambert popped in that 3rd goal from close range yesterday, methinks the die was cast. Those 'Don't Sack Mackay' chants seemed to carry less vigour in the second half as eyes began to open. 'City have only won twelve times in the whole of 2013,' quipped one fan I met in the sweaty environs of the gents' toilets. Hard to argue with him in such circumstances.

At around 4.00 p.m. today the news that Tan had, indeed, lost patience with it all reached me via text, Twitter and all the usual communication channels upon which we now rely. As far as we know, nobody rioted, despite what we had heard continuously in that 45-minute Anfield refrain.

Yet once again, the club managed to handle this badly. Had Tan or the chairman sprinkled the announcement with reference to 'conceded 6 goals in two games ...', ' 3-0 down at half-time in successive matches', 'only two wins since November ...' or even 'that bloke in the bogs thinks Malky is taking the piss', then I think many of the fans might have grudgingly understood. But no, we get talk about 'washing dirty linen in public' and 'personalised arguments'. No mention of the poor run of form or limited impact from big signings such as Odemwingie or Cornelius. So why didn't he 'relieve Malky Mackay of his duties' (to quote the club's website) as soon as this leaked e-mail row erupted then, instead of dragging us all through the mire over our turkey?

Ole Gunnar Solskjær has been installed as favourite to replace Malky. Other names in the hat include Roberto Di Matteo, Glenn Hoddle (??), Sven off of the England job, Dave Jones *(Pah!)* and the aforementioned Turkish guy. Incredibly, Sky Sports even quoted Tan himself at 33-1 to take over. Given his record, this may not be hard to believe as it goes.

We are now presented with another unit of time to add to 'foreseeable future' as the club announce that a new manager will be appointed 'in due course'. We await to see how long that one is.

Ominously, the site also adds chillingly, in red, 'More to follow.' I can well believe it.

Dear Diary,

Saturday, 28 December 2013

Cardiff City 2 – 2 Sunderland

k/o 5.30 p.m.

Vincent Tan and his minions (chairman Mehmet Dalman, chief executive Simon Lim – what do all these people do?)

have spent weeks floating the idea of getting rid of Malky. Then, when they finally do so, they don't have a new manager waiting to come in. Whatever else you might like to say about Tan, the way he runs this club is completely incompetent.

So Malky's number two, David Kerslake, was in charge for this one. I was not expecting a lot, but the players looked 'well up for it'. With Medel back as the midfield anchor, his presence just in front of the defence – from where he did not stray far – allowed Mutch, Kim and Whitts to move around and swap positions. This worked well for about the first 30 minutes of the game, with Kim in particular showing better ball control and passing range than he has previously demonstrated in this league. But we could not add to the excellent Mutch's 6th minute goal – and after those first 30 minutes, Sunderland began to get back into it.

Half-time came at just the right time for us, and in the second half we 'went again'. After 57 minutes, Mutch surged past a couple of Mackem defenders in the inside right channel and put in a low cross with his left foot, which Campbell – having gambled and made the run ahead of his markers – knocked easily into the net from close range. And I said Campbell wouldn't score again from open play – well, he has scored 2 more now, so I was wrong.

(Note for the uninformed: a Mackem is a Sunderland bloke, as a Geordie is a Newcastle one. A Middlesbrough bloke, incidentally, is a Smoggie. And when I say that Campbell 'gambled', I don't mean it in the same sense as Michael Chopra 'gambling' ...)

This goal seemed to effectively kill off the game. But 'seemed' is an ambiguous word. City fell into their old habit of dropping deeper and deeper to protect the lead – invariably this encourages the opposition to come forward, and get back into the game. And so it proved on this occasion. You could also argue that Kerslake's substitutions were no great help, as he took off three of our best players (Noone, Kim and Campbell).

The last came off so we could play Cornelius up front on his own. What this meant was that we played an awful lot of high, hopeful punts to the tall blond Scandinavian. Cornelius proved admirably effective at winning the headers, but as there was nobody playing ahead of him, all his flick-ons did was to deliver possession back to Sunderland much quicker than if he had, say, angled his headers into touch – or if we had just passed the ball around in our own half for a couple of minutes.

Perhaps a better idea might have been to leave Campbell (or Odemwingie, or Maynard, who were both on the bench) up front with the big man, forcing Sunderland to keep more men back. In taking off Noone, our only real ball-carrier, we also gave the visitors less to worry about at the back, allowing them another reason to push more men forward. But we can all be experts after the event, can't we?

And so the inevitable gradually took shape. On 82 minutes, Steven Fletcher got in behind Turner (oo-err), lunged to meet the cross, and steered the ball past Marshall for 2-1. Then the real assault and battery began. It ended in the 95th and final minute, when substitute Jack Colback's shot took the inevitable deflection, which diverted it past Marshall.

And what of Cornelius, the £8 million man who has yet to score for us? He had his chance of a moment of glory from a breakaway in the last few minutes. He galloped down the left with one defender to beat, and did the right thing by trying to cut inside his man – but his attempt looked woefully short of conviction, and the ball got tangled up between his legs. He does not look like a man who is going to score a lot of goals from open play – hang on, though, haven't I said something like that before about someone ... but no, he does not look like £8 million sensibly spent.

As for City, when are we going to win another game? At the moment, it feels like never.

Dear Diary,

Sunday, 29 December 2013

Interesting quote here from City chairman Mehmet Dalman in the *Observer*:

'I am not getting a Turkish manager, I can categorically state. There is a manager who keeps putting himself forward. It is not going to happen.'

So, there we are then.

Dear Diary,

Monday, 30 December 2013

Unlikely source of a news scoop today – Radio Cardiff announced that the players first heard about Malky's sacking via the TV.

I wonder if there might be a PR job going down there in the New Year? I may polish up my CV a little.

Dear Diary,

Tuesday, 31 December 2013

So here we are then, Gareth, New Year's Eve. Old acquaintances and all that. 'Another year over, new one just begun ... but what have we done?'

You're doing that thing when you talk in song lyrics again, aren't you?

'Definitely. Maybe.' ... anyway, what do we think of the year that has gone then, mate? Is Tan a 'scumbag, a maggot, a cheap lousy faggot'? Or is he just 'living in the material world'?

Go on then, I'll bite. On 29 December 2012, we played mighty Millwall at home, gaining a scruffy 1-0 win with a single Rudy Gestede goal after 8 minutes. This year we are looking forward to a run of games which includes Arsenal and both Manchester clubs. Would we have taken that this time last year?

Probably, Gareth, yeah, 'specially if you'd have said we would kick off 2014 outside the PL relegation places, having beaten the Jacks along the way for good measure.

Exactly Dave. 'Seasons in the Sun', eh???

Nice one. I don't think any of us would have seen the sacking of Malky though, would we?

What, even after just one win in the whole of December? We only won once in November remember, and didn't win at all throughout October. Miserable tactics and the most expensive reserve team we have ever had. Miserable shows at Palace and Norwich.

Yeah, yeah, I know, I know. I just wish the club would handle their communications a bit better.

This nonsense of the last few weeks has been an embarrass-ment. 'One Step Beyond', Dave.

Ah well, I am sure 'Things can only get better' in 2014.

'That'll be the day'.

Six

OLE THROUGH THE TRANSFER WINDOW

Dear Diary,

Wednesday, 1 January 2014

Arsenal 2 – 0 Cardiff City

k/o 3.00 p.m.

We have now reached the halfway point of the season, and Arsenal – who we played only four and a half weeks ago in the home game – is our first reverse fixture.

For City, there were two notable debutants. Ole Gunnar Solskjær, heavily rumoured to be the new manager, although not yet actually appointed, appeared in the stand at the Emirates, sat between Vincent 'Dr No' Tan and chairman Dalman. He never looked particularly moved by the events on the pitch, or bore the weighty appearance of a man about to take over the side. He looked more like a bloke who was out for the day on a jolly that somebody else was paying for, and who had a kind of passing interest in football – although not in either of the teams that was playing.

The other newcomer – and this really was *a surprise – was Kevin McNaughton at right-back. With Theo presumably injured (he was not even on the bench), silver-haired Kev, our longest-serving player (signed by Dave Jones in the summer of 2006) was back from his loan spell at Bolton (where he had, in his last game, scored his first goal for six seasons) and in the City side for a debut outing in the Premier League which most of us had feared he would never make.*

Kev struggled for pace at first, but quickly got into the game, and never, from that point on, looked out of place. At one point, he charged down the wing on the overlap, drawing a defender and allowing Noone to cut inside and blast a shot at goal. Not bad for a guy whose play going forward has always been questioned. However, Macca's sudden entree into the side does pose the question, again, of John Brayford, signed from Derby in the summer ('the best full-back in the Championship', as he was heralded at the time) and never played in the Premier. Why was he signed? Who wanted him? If not Malky, and seemingly not Kerslake either, then WHO??! What will happen to him now he has his inevitable three-year contract?

Alright, on with the game. Not much to report here, in truth. City played 4-5-1, so no real change from the Malky mentality. Yes, Campbell played intelligently up front, harrying their defenders. Yes, we closed the Arse down and held them for a long time, and they didn't score until the 87th minute – so another valiant performance.

But did I ever think we would get anything from the game? No, I kind of knew that the home side would score sooner or later. Did we deserve anything from the game? Well, our defensive formation did not allow us much going forward – the cold fact is that we barely troubled the Arse with a shot on target. Defensively, we kept them out for a long time, but a team of Arsenal's quality is very likely to score a goal at some point if they have the 68 per cent possession they enjoyed here.

So a typical City performance, really: essentially negative, seeking to prevent the opponents from playing, but not really doing its job either defensively or offensively. On such foundations are relegations surely built.

In truth, we do not even look very good defensively any more. The back four is often at a dogleg, with no straightness to it, so we cannot catch opponents offside and are having to defend too deep. We have had a manager and assistant this year (Malky and Kerslake) who are both ex-defenders, so how has this been allowed to happen? Caulker is a good pacy centre-back, but is hardly captaincy material – he is not even marshalling his defence properly, let alone talking to the rest of the team. Leadership on the pitch is sorely lacking (this is a department in which we are missing the long-absent Bellamy). All of the defensive uncertainty seems to be affecting the previously solid Turner, who here made a number of mistakes – giving the ball away and failing to go with his man among them. Twice the giant Mertesacker was left unmarked at corners. Although the media will tell us this was a plucky performance, this is not defensive organisation of the highest order.

At no point did we ever try to be positive and put two up front. Nicky Maynard came on, but only in a like-for-like substitution of Campbell, who is starting to appear peeved to be taken off at the 80-minute mark every game. (When he is annoyed, he doesn't look like Gary Wilmot anymore.) We keep doing this 'let's hang on' business, but it rarely seems to work: we must be the worst team in the division for losing points in the last 10 minutes of games. Hang on, we must now be close to being the worst team in the division, full stop – we couldn't even beat Sunderland at home.

We have now won four games from twenty, but three of those were in the first ten games – hence only one win in the last ten. The initial adrenalin (which helped us to beat Man. City and Swansea) has now worn off, and worse than that – opposition managers know what we are about now, and know how to beat us. Something needs to change, and Kerslake offers little different, tactically, to Malky.

I don't know if Ole will be any good or not, but we have more chance of staying up with a new manager, and some fresh ideas on how to get some wins and stay in the division. If we stick with these players and these negative tactics, we will surely go down.

Dear Diary,

Thursday, 2 January 2014

What was slowly becoming the worst kept secret in football finally hit the news today. Here is how the Cardiff City message board broke the news (www.cardiffcity-mad.co.uk):

Cardiff City have appointed Ole Gunnar Solskjær as their new manager.

Solskjær was unveiled as the new Cardiff City boss less than 24 hours after watching his new side lose at Arsenal. He has the honour of trying to manage the football club that has been a point of ridicule because of owner Vincent Tan.

Solskjær was flown by Tan's private jet from Norway to the UK on Wednesday morning and the pair entered The Emirates Stadium together. Ironically Tan, the man who insisted on Cardiff City playing in red, wore a blue shirt to match the away 'Royal' kit the team played in at The Emirates. (The club do not call the change strip blue, just Royal.)

On Thursday just before 1.00 p.m. Solskjær arrived at Cardiff City Stadium and was introduced as the new Cardiff City manager. The 40-year-old Norwegian sat alongside Chairman Mehmet Dalman as he met the press for the first time as Cardiff City manager.

The new boss dismissed claims that Alex Ferguson tried to dissuade him from taking the Cardiff job.

'That is absolute nonsense,' said Solskjær. 'He has wished me the best and given me some good advice as he always does. I had a good conversation with him.'

Solskjær was a star striker for Manchester United under Ferguson and scored the winning goal in the 1999 Champions League final. As an attacker he likes to bring an attack minded approach to his management. Something that might help avoid the second half rearguard display at The Emirates.

'It is a fantastic challenge. Cardiff are ready to take the next step up. I hope I can help them,' Solskjær said. 'I've always dreamt of being a manager in the Premier League and I'm delighted to get the opportunity.'

Dear Diary,

Friday, 3 January 2014

A combination of the lure of the PL and the newsworthiness of landing a big name manager has, not for the first time this season, focused national media attention onto events at Cardiff City. No opportunity is missed either, of course, to inject some Fergie references into the story of how City have recruited a United legend to the Bluebirds' hot seat.

The *Guardian* devoted three pages to such events today. Reporter, Stuart James, conducted a somewhat 'harsh but fair' analysis of Cardiff City FC against criteria set by Fergie himself for accepting any managerial post.

James felt that the club easily met the first of these criteria, 'is it a good club' *(??)*, but failed on the second, 'does it have a good history'. He gave us the benefit of the doubt as to the extent of financial leeway available to the new boss but, for the fourth criterion – does the club have a chairman who 'understands the game', James' verdict was simply a resounding 'No Way!'

Like I say, harsh but fair perhaps.

Dear Diary,

Saturday, 4 January 2014

Newcastle United 1 – 2 Cardiff City

k/o 3.00 p.m.

I was a bit pissed off about this, to be honest.

Here we are, in the middle of a relegation battle, with wins few and far between, and we go and 'waste' a precious victory on the FA Cup – hardly our priority this year, is it?

Yeah, I know the extra confidence will do us all the world of good – but will it? New managers often have an immediate impact, but sometimes it's quite brief. A team will generally be 'fired up' for one game, but often the impact only lasts for one game – and this may have been it.

How did City perform? Well, new boss 'Saltshaker' did not shake things up too much, sticking with the tired and tested 4-5-1 formation, although Cornelius (largely ineffectual, I'm afraid) was given the starting berth up front. Club captain Mark Hudson came into central defence for Caulker, and also took over the skipper's duties for the day.

City showed admirable grit to battle back from 1–0 down at the break. The goals? Craig Noone scored with a wonder shot from outside the box, and Fraizer Campbell headed in the winner from close range from a corner. But City did not create an awful lot more than those two chances, and they beat a Magpies side who had seven regular starters missing.

City still need to make three good signings to stay up. A win in the Cup is nothing like a win in the League.

And City badly, badly need another one of those.

Gareth, take one of me looking for our seats ...

Dear Diary,
Monday, 6 January 2014

No entry yesterday, thanks to jet lag (well, coach lag then) after that marathon trek north. Unsurprisingly, the media was full of cheer today; tales of 'Super Subs', 'unexpected FA Cup fixtures against Bolton' and new tactical dawns. But, amidst the reference to unpronounceable potential Scandinavian signings, we find, tucked away in the inside of the local press, an interesting quote from our new gaffer. 'You try to learn about the club's history because that is important to the fans,' he states.

Do you think he will wear a blue scarf at matches, like Mancini used to do at Man. City?

Dear Diary,
Wednesday, 8 January 2014

Full marks to the poster who posted 'it's a Wolff, it's a Wolff' on the CCMB today, in response to our forthcoming signing of Magnus Wolff Eikrem from Ole's former club Molde in Norway. Bonus points to Cwmbran's 'SparkyMark' for spotting that we now have a wolf, a pit bull and a Great Dane in the side ...

Sadly, none of the 4,000 plus people who viewed this post really got the joke – all failed to make the connection by highlighting that we are also due to sign the Yemeni striker Lambsi.

Dear Diary,
Thursday, 9 January 2014

In other news, former Aston Villa midfielder Thomas Hitzlsperger has been speaking further today about his announcement yesterday that he was gay. The 52 times capped German international is the most prominent footballer to publicly reveal his homosexuality and said that it was 'a good time' to do so.

He was quoted as saying that 'hopefully if some players follow, one day it will become normal and not big news anymore.'

Good on him, I say.

Dear Diary,

Friday, 10 January 2014

Now I am not great with figures.

I know the difference between a size 8 and a size 16, and I understand the flat back four and how away-goals count double in the event of a tie. But real sums, well they leave me a bit cold to be honest.

So I may struggle with this bit. But Cardiff City today recorded a £30 million loss in their latest set of financial accounts – taking their overall debt to an eye-watering £118 million. Imagine owing someone £118 million??

Anyway, within these figures, £66 million is owed to Vincent Tan from loans to the club, despite the high-trousered one converting £2.5 million into shares and writing off £5 million in interest. The accounts, which record the financial period up to last May, also confirm that life president Sam Hammam's Langston was paid £22 million to solve the historic debt it was owed. Naming rights seem to have been dispensed with as part of this settlement.

My schooldays in Tremorfa didn't really prepare me for all this, but I will keep going ...

The club's wages and salaries jumped from £18.5 million in 2012, to almost £30 million in 2013, while revenue fell from £20 million in 2012 to just over £17 million in 2013. Not sure how that works. I thought our crowds were bigger? Unless it's a Carling Cup thing.

Fortunately Cardiff City Supporters Trust paid more attention during maths lessons than I did, and their guys seem to understand this mumbo jumbo. Board member and accountant Keith Morgan queries, for example, why non-footballing costs have gone up so hugely.

'Administration doesn't include players' wages so why the hell have they gone up from £7 million to £15 million?' he asks.

'It doesn't explain anywhere in the notes why the non-footballing costs have just about doubled. It is still the same stadium as it was before, still the same number of stadium staff so what is in there?' He also throws the issue of income from SKY into the mix.

I reckon TV income should probably offset some of this expenditure by the time next year's accounts are published, but isn't that putting all your eggs in one basket a little? And what does all this 'converting debt into equity' stuff mean?

This season is rapidly growing into one very long headache ...

Dear Diary,

Saturday, 11 January 2013

Cardiff City 0 – 2 West Ham United

k/o 3.00 p.m.

My worst fears were confirmed after the Newcastle win, and City were well and truly dumped 'back in the mire' by this clunking defeat.

West Ham can't score, and were here without Andy Carroll, Kevin Nolan and Joe Cole – the players most likely to. So what happens? The visitors nearly hit the back of the net within 5 minutes, first rattling the post, then forcing Marshall into making a smart save. Carlton Cole – a player we could have signed on a free last summer – was a handful throughout. At the back, the away side featured debutant new signing Roger Johnson, a player many City supporters were keen to see come back here – but in our colours rather than theirs ...

City were not totally abject. We briefly threatened. Odemwingie, who generally had another terrible game, enjoyed one good moment, dribbling through a couple of attempted tackles before pulling the ball back from the byline. Noone had a chance to shoot, but he was desperate to get it on his left, and by the time he had taken his extra touch, a West Ham defender was there to block the effort. (Oh for two-footed wingers ... but, of course, the players are so much better (sic) these days, aren't they?)

A few minutes before half-time, West Ham broke, Carlton Cole beat Caulker all ends up, and nearly scored. Somehow we survived, but little good did it do us, as Cole bundled the ball home from Matt Jarvis's cross a few moments later.

Saltshaker immediately shook things up by bringing on Bellamy at half-time. Bellers looked livelier than hitherto, and we certainly looked sharper for his introduction – but often he was taking the ball directly from his defenders, and in general he played so deep that he was never really going to trouble the visitors in the area of the pitch where we needed him to. The same goes for Magnus Wolff Eikrem, Ole's new Norwegian midfielder, who knocked the ball around nicely – but again, just in front of the defence, where all our midfielders (Mutch honourably excepted) seem to want to play.

At the start of the season, we couldn't play the ball out of defence, and kept losing it. Now, we can knock it around for long periods, but in almost totally predictable directions. Nobody seems to try to quickly switch the play, and 90 per cent of the passes are sideways or backwards. We really needed to make some quality signings to give us a chance of staying up, but Saltshaker seems only to want to sign fellow Norsemen. Are they going to be any better than what we've already got?

Our best chance in the second half was a Caulker header from a corner, which was cleared off the line. We are still playing one up front (at home, against a poor team), and we are still only looking like scoring from set pieces. Plus ça change! With 20 minutes to go, Hammers centre-back, James Tomkins, was sent off for a second yellow (a high kick, deemed dangerous), and the crowd erupted with a massive cheer, as if somebody had just scored the winner. We still needed 2 goals to win the damn game!

We rarely looked like getting either of them, even though Ole made a positive change by bringing off a defender (Hudson) for an extra attacker. Unfortunately, our extra attacker was Cornelius, so the additional goal threat was decidedly minimal. It all brings back my mate's phrase that you can't really change anything by shuffling and reshuffling a bad pack – and this is the unfortunate part of Malky's legacy. A team nowhere near good enough for the Premier League.

The 'ammers sealed our fate minutes from the end when, with City committed to attack, they broke down the right. Carroll fed a nicely weighted inside ball to the experienced Mark Noble, and the midfielder calmly slotted the ball past Marshall and inside the far post.

So City fell into the bottom three for the first time. Can we get back out? Sadly, with Palace continuing to revive and Sunderland today winning 4–1 at Fulham, we are now starting to look like the worst team in the division.

Dear Diary,
Sunday, 12 January 2014

Today's League table:

		P	W	D	L	F	A	Diff	Pts
	West Ham United	21	4	6	11	21	30	−9	18
18	Cardiff City	21	4	6	11	15	34	−19	18
19	Sunderland	21	4	5	12	19	34	−15	17
20	Crystal Palace	21	5	2	14	13	31	−18	17

Like I say, one big headache.

Dear Diary,
Monday, 13 January 2014

Somewhat against our better judgement perhaps, Gareth and I have booked with 'TIT tours' (Tony's Independent Travel) to travel to Manchester City on Saturday, £75 all in – they even pick up in Pentwyn.

See you at 7.20 a.m. Gareth ...

Dear Diary,
Thursday, 16 January 2014

A worrying time for the overworked spell checker looms, as we discover today that the Bluebirds have snatched 'Mats Møller Dæhli' from Molde FK. I am afraid I know little more about this lad, other than he is described as a talented 18-year-old playmaker.

Dave, what exactly is a 'playmaker'?
Pass.

Dear Diary,

Saturday, 18 January 2014

Manchester City 4 – 2 Cardiff City

k/o 3.00 p.m.

Gareth has passed the match journalist's pen to me today. He tells me that he has writer's cramp, but I think the fact that we started drinking at 8.00 a.m. may have something to do with his recollection of events.

The Etihad Stadium does not disappoint. Like a giant space ship, it seems to have landed smack in the middle of Manchester, sucking in the natives with its giant force. 'Close Encounters of the Moss Side'.

Manchester City are, of course, the Galacticos of the Premier League. Scorers of goals a-plenty and boasting a string of star names. We, by comparison, switched Kevin McNaughton to left-back. We hadn't kept a clean sheet at Manchester City for ninety years.

The nightmare start we all feared almost manifested itself in the opening minutes, as Naughts came flying through in characteristic fashion and was relatively fortunate not to be penalised for an ungainly looking challenge in the heart of our penalty area. We held our breath, but no penalty.

Actually we managed to hold our breath for a good 10 minutes or so, before David Silva grabbed possession from a quickly taken throw-in. Silva shuffled and wriggled his way into the box – with the aid of a shove on the ball from his upper arm perhaps – before finding Edin Dzeko who scuffed the ball over the line, despite Kev's attempted clearance from behind the goal line, and a hint of another handball. This became the first ever PL goal to be awarded thanks to goal line technology. Geoff Hurst, eat your heart out.

Despite being somewhat outplayed in this encounter, City remained in contention. After 29 minutes Craig Noone jinked forward, cut inside, slipped his way around Victor Kompany and then hooked his shot past England's Joe Hart in the Man. City goal. Amazingly, City were level. Bemused silence in the home seats. Bedlam in ours.

I must admit, there was a chunk of this first half that seemed to pass me by, thanks to an ungainly spell of rumpus in the away end. From what I could gather – and this took place only a few feet away from me – a steward had taken offence to some bad language from a City fan. This resulted in an attempted ejection, which met with resistance, to say the least. More stewards arrived. City reinforcements joined the affray. For a while things became quite ugly, as police, stewards and a mob of Cardiff fans all bundled, shoved and congregated in a messy tangle over the seats. A steward was floored as things intensified. You'll never ban a City fan apparently. 'Are you fighting over sheep?' sang the home fans. Very witty, I am sure.

Back on the pitch, the natural order had been restored following some loose play by Caulker (again) as Jesus Navas restored the home side's advantage with their 101st goal of the season. Frightening. I know Man. City are good, but at times this season our defending has been criminally naïve.

Despite the Mancunians' extra quality, the Bluebirds stuck at it deep into the second half. Bellamy and Declan John joined the proceedings. Noone remained a constant threat.

With around a quarter of an hour to go though, the massive Yaya Touré's patience clearly became exhausted. The giant African simply eased up through the gears before smashing the ball past a helpless Marshall. Moments later Aguero made it 4 as our deep fears began to materialise. 'You've had your laff; now f**k off home,' sang the relaxed home fans, late in the game.

But Man of the Match, Noone, was having none of it, forcing a sprawling one-handed save from Hart. From the resulting 90th-minute corner, Fraizer Campbell bundled in his 6th goal of the season – his 3rd against Manchester City. A cue for the Poznan in the away end – but a cue for a new name at the bottom of this year's Premier League table.

Dear Diary,
Sunday, 19 January 2014

So yesterday's defeat, plus the results of other games, puts City on the bottom of the table, though only by goal difference.

Ole remains optimistic: 'At times yesterday we looked like a proper team.'

Shit – were we as bad as that under Malky??

Dear Diary,

Tuesday, 21 January 2014

As things currently seem a little quiet on the CCFC transfer rumour mill (though we hear constant talk of Wilf Zaha coming on loan from United), there was time to look beyond our own shallow waters a little today. And we hear that, way out west, the waters may be growing somewhat choppy ...

Apparently, the board of Swansea City are mindful of a growing crisis as Michael Laudrup admits that the club are facing 'dark days'. Police were called to the training ground after Chico Flores was allegedly spotted threatening Garry Monk with a brick during training. Swansea's players are also understood to be fed up with training, and results have shown a desperate dip in form which has plunged them towards the relegation zone. Hopefully this should all put them in the right frame of mind for 8 February.

Laudrup's relationship with the Swansea chairman is supposedly at breaking point but, as he has seventeen months left on his contract, it would cost them around £4 million to pay him off in the summer – according to the *Daily Mirror*'s website.

Malky for Swansea, anyone?

Brrrrrrrrrrhhhh ...

(Dave, remind me again, why are we interested in this Swansea lot??)

Dear Diary,

Thursday, 23 January 2014

Aaaaagh!! The Premier League want to prosecute pubs in South Wales who are showing matches illegally. This could make a serious dent in our football-watching habits.

Dear Diary,

Friday, 24 January 2014

We still wait on Zaha, then. All seems likely to go ahead but maybe not in time for the FA Cup trip to Bolton tomorrow. City are also linked with Molde midfielder Jo Inge Berget.

Another midfield player, Dave???

Hey, don't shoot me, I am only the piano player. We are also after Wigan centre-back, Ivan Ramis, apparently.

That can't be right, mate – he is not Norwegian after all.

Dear Diary,

Saturday, 25 January 2014

Bolton Wanderers 0 – 1 Cardiff City

(FA Cup 4)

k/o 3.00 p.m.

We took the field with a slightly weakened side, with Hudson and Cornelius both given another run out (they had played in the previous round at Newcy). Alas, Cornelius showed little improvement, and was hauled off at half-time.

Very little of any note occurred in the first half. After the break, Ole introduced Noone and Campbell, and things livened up a bit. The two combined for the only goal of the game 5 minutes later, though this was largely due to a fumble from Trotters keeper Andy Lonergan. He dropped Noone's cross in front of Campbell, who was in the right place at the right time to knock the ball in. (Question: given that Campbell was in the right place at the right time, could he have been in the right place at the wrong time? Answer: suppose so. Or even the wrong place at the right time? How about the wrong place at the wrong time???)

Teenage midfield playmaker Mats Møller Dæhli came on for the last 15 minutes, and showed some nice touches. A few minutes from time, he made an excellent jinking run and shot. The boy can play!

The sour notes were the mediocre performances of Cornelius and Eikrem, who was ineffectual as the midfield anchor man, and went off with 'Corny' at the break. Was his West Ham cameo a mere illusion?

Better news is coming in, though. Having perhaps secured, in the shape of 'Arfur' Dæhli, the penetrating player we need on the left, we are now, apparently, about to sign Kenwyne Jones from Stoke. He may well be the experienced target man that we have been desperately short of all season. In addition, he is supposed to be coming in exchange for Odemwingie, who has been – apart from some early fleeting moments – awful since joining us.

This deal, if it comes off, is a great bit of business by Ole. There is still talk, too (in the national press, not the Echo*) that the much sought after Wilfried Zaha is going to join us. Dæhli, Kenwyne and Zaha – three decent attacking signings. If two of the three come off, we have a decent chance of staying up.*

Oh, and we are also through to the 5th round of the Cup. Almost forgot to mention that ...

Dear Diary,
Sunday, 26 January 2014

Now, I know I have a mild hangover after yesterday's Burns Night Party, but I am feeling somewhat confused today. For Ole is supposed to be going all attack-minded after the slightly more 'cautious' approach favoured by Malky, yet he criticises our new Boy Wonder, Dæhli, whom he sent on near the end yesterday with a little dig at the midfield player, saying: 'He tried to shoot – and we'd told him to pass rather than shoot!'

He also thinks we can actually win the cup.

Mind you – with United already out, Chelsea facing a tough trip to the Etihad and Liverpool drawn against Arsenal, the draw is looking good for us. A home tie against holders Wigan in the 5th round looks pretty winnable. We could be in the quarter finals at this rate.

I wonder if there is time to bring out a 'Secret Diary of an FA Cup Run?'

Dear Diary,

Monday, 27 January 2014

I mean, really. Really. You couldn't make it up, could you? Check this diary entry when you read it to make sure it isn't 1 April, for, in another amazing development at Cardiff City Football Club, we now understand that our friend Mr Tan has been taking football advice from ... Dave Jones.

Yes, THAT Dave Jones.

Apparently Jones has become close to Vincent Tan and has been offering advice on running the club. F**k no! It was Tan who actually sacked Jones in May 2011 but it is now claimed that he was in favour of keeping him, and the *rest* of the board decided to axe him!! Jones endorsed current boss Ole Gunnar Solskjær as the man to succeed Malky Mackay, and his friend-ship with Tan has helped him make decisions on the running of the club.

To put it mildly, it is something of a surprise to see Jones back and involved even in an informal capacity. Jones has also been to stay in with Tan, and they have developed a strong friendship and 'working relationship'.

Malky must be scratching his head at that one.

Dear Diary,

Tuesday, 28 January 2014

Manchester United 2 – 0 Cardiff City

k/o 7.45 p.m.

Saltshaker sprang a few more selection surprises on us for this game. McNaughton now reverted to his favourite position of right-back (for Theo), with Declan John returning at left-back. Hudson was preferred to Turner in central defence. Bellamy returned on the left-wing against one of his former clubs, with Whitts returning to central midfield, and Gunnarsson omitted. United had Juan Mata making his debut, and Robin Van Persie just back from injury – so we did not get much luck with the timing of this game.

We made a poor start, with United – who have struggled at home, even against mediocre sides – getting their first goal within 6 minutes. Ashley Young put over a cross which Valencia – who had ghosted inside off his wing (when do City wingers do that?) – headed against the bar. Van Persie, unmarked (!) at the far post, headed the rebound, which Marshall somehow managed to keep out. But 'RVP' was still given enough time and space by the City defenders to head in the second (!!) rebound.

(Funny story: when the Arse signed Van Persie, whose middle name is Simon, they were actually after another player. They sent an e-mail to Feyenoord saying, 'We are interested in one of your players RSVP ...')

Okay, on with the game. City managed to get into it, and by half-time they had managed to carve out a couple of (half) chances. Craig Noone was enjoying another good game on the 'big occasion' (wonder if he will still be with us next season!), causing Evra plenty of problems. After 35 minutes, he drifted inside, cleverly creating space for McNaughton outside him. The Silver Fox got a decent cross in, but City had nobody on the end of it. As has happened too often this season, there was a lack of our bodies in the opposition box. 4-5-1 might work for some teams, but it doesn't seem to do us a lot of favours.

City cause themselves problems, though, with players having 'nosebleeds'. Whittingham seems to have developed a nosebleed over making forward passes. Everything he hits now has to go sideways or backwards – I am afraid it has become a compulsion. At one point, City were attacking from a set piece, so had many players forward. The ball came to Whitts, and he turned back and passed to Medel – who was already marked by a United attacker! Yet Whitts has played in every game this season, is our only League ever-present, and has only once even been substituted. Surely, with all the new signings coming in, Whitts has to be the first to go ...?

Bellers, alas, has also developed a nosebleed problem. He has a nosebleed if he thinks about trying to beat anybody. After 40 minutes, City counter-attacked, and had a 2 v. 2 situation high up the pitch. Mutch peeled away, taking one of the defenders with him, so Bellers only had to beat one man and get a shot in. But he looked petrified at the prospect, instead feeding Mutch, who was still marked. I am afraid there is no point picking Bellers if he won't even try to beat the man, so he is another who has to go.

After the break, City had lots of possession, but rarely looked like troubling United. The one occasion they did came when Declan John overlapped on the left. He reached the byline and pulled the ball back – unfortunately just behind Campbell, who was racing in at the near post. United managed to clear the ball.

Campbell managed a shot from another City attack soon after, but all City's pressure came to naught (not 'Naught'!) when United hit us with a sucker punch on the break. The ball was fed to Young on the left. Young, who is very right-footed, likes to come inside, but McNaughton and Noone unfortunately allowed him to do exactly this, and he curled a clinical shot past Marshall and inside the far post. Game over.

So City are at the bottom with 18 points from twenty-three games (well behind Malky's 1 point per game ratio), and only fifteen games left. Ole has brought in six new signings in the transfer window, but the question is: are they any better, or at least different, from what we have got? Three of them are Norwegians who have not played at this level before, so 'the jury is out' on them. My suspicion with Dæhli, who came on as a sub at Old Trafford, is that he has been signed 'for the future' – unfortunately, we need results NOW. Eikrem did not figure here, and Ole has gone back to the tired and trusted duo of Medel and Whitts in central midfield – who have created virtually nothing between them all season.

The other three we have signed are Fabio, Zaha (on loan) and Kenwyne Jones. The Fabio deal bemuses me. Do we need a left-back? I thought Declan was fine. Is Fabio any better than Declan? The Brazilian has done nothing in the Premier League, and United only signed him in the first place to 'hold Rafael's hand', as the twins could not be separated. Perhaps United told us we could only sign Zaha if we agreed to take Fabio as well.

Zaha offers us penetration down the left, which we have not enjoyed all season. But he is a player who did well in the

Championship – so we have no idea if he can do it in the Prem. But at least he was worth a shot.

Kenwyne offers us the chance of a decent target man, which we have lacked all season due to Malky's imbecilic decision to sign Cornelius, and no other 'number 9'. He has done well in this league before. The problem is, we have signed him on a permanent deal – a loan deal would have been better, as that may have given him the incentive to perform well. As he has secured his contract already, will he be motivated to 'turn it on' for us? Time will tell.

The problem is, there is not much time. Our next four games are Norwich (home), Swansea (away), Villa (home) and Hull (home). We do not have many 'winnable' games in our last fifteen, and these four all fall into that category. I feel we need to win three of them to stay up. For a side with only four victories all season, it is a 'big ask' ...

Dear Diary,
Wednesday, 29 January 2014

'I read the news today, oh boy ...'

Even by this season's standards, even by Cardiff City's standards, this was a bonkers day. Look at these stories, from just one day ... in the life of Cardiff City:

Andreas Cornelius is set to return to FC Copenhagen after failing to make an impact in South Wales. Stories suggest we are letting him go for £3 million – thus making a loss of around £8 million on the deal.

Joe Mason has joined Bolton Wanderers on loan but a bid from the Trotters for Kevin McNaughton is turned down.

Keeper Simon Moore looks set for a loan move to Bristol City.

On Saturday, we look set to field a Brazilian full-back, a centre forward from Trinidad & Tobago, a winger on loan from Man U, a Chilean, some Norwegians, possibly an Icelander ... and a defender from Merthyr Tydfil.

Cardiff City are now two wins away from safety, following a rare dose of Premier League midweek fixtures.

For the first time in most people's memory, Cardiff City's next home game is a direct clash with a Six Nations home game. There are a mere 150 tickets left.

... and twenty years ago today, Nathan Blake scored that winner against Man. City at Ninian Park. That's the same Man. City who won away 5–1 at Spurs today to go top of the league. They have scored 51 more goals than us in the league alone.

Dear Diary,
Friday, 31 January 2014

In another eventful day (yes, another one), the transfer window slammed shut this evening at 11.00 p.m. The rumour mill almost blew a gasket, as Cardiff City found themselves chasing, or linked with, a host of big names. Cissé (Newcastle), Le Fondre (Reading) and even Ross McCormack from Leeds. None of these actually came off, but we do now have our first Trinidad and Tobagan (how can you be from two countries?), alongside Fabio (who goes by just the one name, like Sting, Madonna and Sooty) and Wilf Zaha. I can't wait to shout 'Go on, Wilfried' at a match soon, something I never thought I would find myself saying.

Ex-City stars enjoyed mixed fortunes on this eventful evening. Joe Ledley cashed in his chips at Celtic and will now turn out for relegation rivals Crystal Palace, along with Wales' keeper Wayne Hennessy, while our old mate Darcy Blake has had his contract terminated at Palace by mutual consent. Another City old boy, Brian McDermott, featured in the most bizarre sequence of events as the Leeds United website announced that, despite the rumours, their manager was going nowhere, only for Sky Sports (where would we be on transfer deadline day without Sky Sports??) to confirm his sacking moments later. Back at the Cardiff City Stadium, we also hear tales of a bid for Spanish Under-19 centre-half Juan Carla, the 24-year-old former Sevilla player, who would be available outside of the transfer window as a free agent.

Amidst all this ballyhoo, the news of the enormous hike in season ticket prices could easily have been missed. I have read of a 15 per cent increase in some cases. You could be forgiven for thinking that the club had deliberately chosen this busy news day to sneak this information out, couldn't you ...?

Seven

MY FUNNY VALENTINE

Dear Diary,

Saturday, 1 February

Cardiff City 2 – 1 Norwich City

k/o 3.00 p.m.

I hesitate to use the expression 'must-win game'. If a game is a 'must-win', what happens if we don't? Is the season over?

Well, despite my hesitation, this was an 'almost-must-win game'. Because if we couldn't win this one, with all the new signings, playing at home, against a struggling team, then when would we ever win?

Ole put Kenwyne Jones straight into the side as the lone striker, replacing the luckless Fraizer Campbell. Having toiled on his own all season, the Gary Wilmot lookalike finally found a potential partner in crime – only to immediately lose his place to him!

Mutch and Bellamy, rather oddly, swapped roles. Mutch was shunted out to the left, where he rarely looked comfortable, and Bellamy stuck in 'the hole', where, in truth, he did very little. Despite all the signings, Ole still stuck with Medel and Whitts in central midfield. Hmmm ...

There were two changes to the defence. Fabio was apparently signed as a right-back, not a left-back – so we now have five of these! (Count 'em: Fabio, Theo, Naughts, Brayford and Connolly.)

It was amazing that we managed to win this game. As at Old Trafford, we conceded a goal within the first 6 minutes. This time, Canaries left-back Martin Olsson overlapped and crossed into the box, where Bradley Johnson (unmarked) stabbed the ball home from close range. For most of the first half, we were awful, constantly losing possession in our own half, as the new-look team struggled to find their shape.

Another factor playing havoc with City was the strong wind. They kept trying to play from the back – but Norwich seemed to be far more effective in dealing with the wind than we were. All we did was lose the ball all the time.

Finally, City got wise to the conditions, and Marshall came up to take a free-kick near the halfway line, which he was able to loft into the Norwich box – but it came to naught. Then Medel won a tackle (one of many he won this afternoon), Noone got the ball and cut inside and put in a dangerous cross which just eluded Mutch, ghosting in at the far post. Alas, this was about the only time that Mutch did anything from the left midfield berth.

The Norwich fans, who were loud throughout, started chanting 'You should've gone to the rugby!', and for about 40 minutes, I was thinking they were right. Then Ole took the miraculous decision, after 38 minutes, to take off the woefully ineffective Whittingham – who was audibly jeered off by the boo-boys. Mutch moved into the middle, and debut-making substitute Wilfried Zaha went out left – and made an immediate impact. We could soon see that Zaha was a player who wanted to run at people – and for the first time this season, we had a ball-carrier on both flanks.

City put some sustained pressure on Norwich for the first time, but at the interval had still not managed to carve out a clear-cut chance.

The second half got underway, and within minutes, Norwich had gifted us a goal. Canaries striker, Gary Hooper, played a crazy ball across his own penalty area, straight to Zaha (who had come in off his wing to harass the defenders). Because the ball had been given away so high up the pitch, Bellamy was – for about the only time in the game – in their penalty area. He made an intelligent run between the defenders, Zaha found him, and Bellers managed to slip it under the body of the visiting keeper, John Ruddy.

Suddenly City were swarming all over them. Norwich looked as if they didn't know what had hit them. Within 1 minute of the equaliser, the ball was fed to Mutch, who had momentarily swapped positions with Noone. Mutch crossed, Kenwyne got up and headed it towards goal. Ruddy's strong hand kept it out, but Kenwyne looked hungrier than the defenders, and he reacted quickest to blast home the rebound. (... almost landing on my lap with his somersault goal celebration, by the way.)

Somehow City had got their noses in front. But their attacking burst soon petered out, and they spent the rest of the game trying, in predictable fashion, to hang on. Ole, having pulled off a decisive attacking substitution in the first half, now fell for the same mistake as Malky, taking off a creative midfielder (Mutch) and putting on a defensive one (Gunnarsson). We now had Medel and Gunnar in central midfield – there was no passer, and so we could not keep possession for very long. A bad idea! Our experience this season has surely demonstrated that the best way to defend is to keep the bloody ball. And, to use a military expression, the best form of defence is attack. When we try to 'kill' a game, we just can't do it.

The last 15 minutes were a nightmare. Norwich had already hit the crossbar, when Marshall superbly deflected a goal-bound shot upwards. Now they hit the woodwork again, had two goals disallowed for offside, and had another two efforts stopped by superb saves from Marshy.

The final whistle at last blew, and somehow City had won. We scored with just about our only two real chances, while Norwich had about ten chances and scored once. But we also used up all our luck for the rest of the season in one game. A win is a win, and this could be the start of a fight back – but we have got to play better than this if we are going to win in Jackland.

NB: Bellers' goal – his first of the season – meant that he became the first player to score for seven different clubs in the Premier League. That's a good seven-point question in a pub quiz! Kenwyne's scoring effort was also his first Premier goal for over a year.

Dear Diary,
Sunday, 2 February 2014

Leeds have reinstated McDermott! (She loves me, she loves me not ...)

In other news, we read that Vincent Tan has also reinstated his visits to the Cardiff City dressing room and even popped in on Saturday during half-time to give the lads a piece of his mind.

Judging by the second-half improvement, maybe he should do that more often ...

Dear Diary,
Monday, 3 February 2014

Bit of an 'eyebrow raiser' in my inbox today. For Malky Mackay has accepted an invitation to become an honorary member of Cardiff City Supporters' Trust. The trust chief, Tim Hartley, was understandably pleased to release this news. Malky described how it was an 'absolute pleasure' to receive the trust's invitation and how he 'absolutely loved' his time in Cardiff.

I am not so sure about this. I know we all enjoyed the two-year love affair with Malky, but if the trust are aiming to gain the ear and confidence of Vincent Tan, I wouldn't have thought that siding with his old flame is the way to go about it.

Don't expect a Valentine's Day card from Tan at this rate, Tim.

Dear Diary,
Tuesday, 4 February 2014

'Anything you can do ...'

Not to be outdone, our friends down west sacked their manager, Michael Laudrup, last night. The Jacks have been lacklustre for almost a year, to be honest, since winning the Whatever-it's-called Cup last year. Didn't quite expect this, though. Another shattered romance.

Gary-Who?-Monk had been put in charge, just days ahead of their clash with us, together with Swans' legend Alan Curtis.

I don't like the sound of this, if I am honest. I was quite happy with the Swans slipping into disarray under Laudrup, but this is just the sort of twist that could galvanise them against us.

Dear Diary,

Friday, 7 February 2014

For the second week running, a Cardiff City game is to take place in a direct 'head-to-head' clash with international rugby. Well, almost.

For many years, those amongst us who care little for the fate of the egg-chasers have usually simply just retreated into our shell each January/February, while the daffodil-and-cowboy-hat–wearing hordes yell 'Go on Shane' at the TV.

This year, though, the balance may be switching. City's attendance for last week's game against Norwich topped 26,000; while the attendance across the city for Wales' rugby match against Italy that afternoon failed to fill the Millennium Stadium by some distance. Tonight's *South Wales Echo* also carried page upon page of coverage of this weekend's big derby, while the rugby clash in Ireland was buried deep within the sports' section, some way from the prestigious back page itself.

I still don't get the whole 'Six Nations' thing, mind. I thought Ireland was made up of two countries. Mind you, the Winter Olympics started today too, and we are expected to cheer on a team calling themselves 'GB', which wouldn't include Northern Ireland usually, so what do I know?

Dear Diary,

Saturday, 8 February 2014

Swansea City 3 – 0 Cardiff City

k/o 3.00 p.m.

This was a horrible game (for us!), played in awful conditions – driving rain and wind – and with an equally awful outcome.

The eyes of the world are on us. (God, please don't let us blow it.)

In truth, we lost this game before the start, with a truly horrendous team selection from Ole. Out went Noone and Mutch – our only talented attackers – in favour of Kim, who has done very little in the Premier League, and Zaha, who was able to do very little today. Yet again we left one striker to toil on his own up front.

Ole seems now merely to be replicating the errors of Malky, who began the season with neither Mutch nor Noone in the team. He eventually realised he needed them both if City were to create anything. Now Ole (who has seemingly not watched many of our games!) is about to go through exactly the same learning process. Managers, eh? Don't you just love 'em?

Oh, I should have mentioned that Whitts retained his place in the team. Despite Ole's 'brave' decision to take him off before half-time in the previous game, the boss apparently did not have the bravery to then omit him from the team for the next game. This is rather reminiscent of Dave Jones and Lee Naylor ...

We almost conceded another early goal for the third game running. Jacks' debutant, Marvin Emnes, who has caused problems for us in the past, broke through, but Marshall saved. Then Bony nearly scored – which reminds me, both teams had a Wilfried on the pitch – bizarre or what?

Enough of the esoterica, on with the game.

City hit back, got some possession, and created a couple of half chances. Bellers turned Britton and put in a cross towards Kenwyne, but Flores' challenge was enough to force the big Trinidadian to misdirect his header well wide. Then Bellers played a one-two with Declan and crossed, but Kenwyne stabbed the ball past the post. Bellers, clearly fired up for the occasion, was doing what he had signally failed to do all season: attack the space with speed and menacing intent.

City had more chances, with shots from Bellers and Whitts, but couldn't score. There was hope for the second half, but this was crushed within a minute when Swansea took a largely undeserved lead. Pablo Hernandez, who had come on as a half-time sub, played a clever ball into space behind Fabio, who was caught flat-footed and out of position. Routledge raced into space, and Marshall oddly opted to remain on his line (his second mistake of the season?), allowing the winger an easy chance to advance and knock the ball past him, and inside the far post: 1-0 to the Jacks.

We had one response to this, when an infuriated Bellamy cut into the Swansea area and lashed a vicious, curling shot which smacked against the crossbar and bounced to safety. And, as far as City were concerned, that was that.

Dyer nearly scored another for the Jacks after Caulker kept backing off him. Then later, Turner pulled off the same trick, backing off Hernandez, despite the fact that he was the only attacker, up against three defenders. Why do we keep backing off in these situations? We have been doing it all season. Do they practise anything in training??

With a dozen minutes to go, Swansea sealed it when Routledge crossed from the left and Dyer, coming off the opposite wing, sneaked in front of Declan John, who was 'ball-watching', to nod the ball past Marshall. An elementary error, but Declan will get better. On full time, a thoroughly miserable evening was rounded off when, from a Swansea free-kick, Bony got above Turner to nod the ball in for 3-0 – the heaviest South Wales derby defeat for some years.

Despite the poor team selections, there was some promise, but it ended up looking very grim indeed. Relegation is looking like a more and more ominous prospect.

Dear Diary,

Sunday, 9 February 2014

Gareth – do you fancy an overnight trip to Bournemouth next season?

Dear Diary,

Tuesday, 11 February 2014

Cardiff City 0 – 0 Aston Villa

k/o 7.45 p.m.

After his terrible team selection for the Swansea game, Ole performed a miraculous about-turn for this game, and brought back all the players he should have picked at the Liberace Stadium.

Theo came back at right-back for the not-very-good Fabio, who had to be substituted in both his games. Noone was back on the right (for Kim), and Mutch came into central midfield to partner Medel, Whittingham being justifiably omitted. Zaha started again, so that three of our midfield quartet were attacking players. And, for the first time this season, we started with two proper strikers, Campbell coming into the side to partner Kenwyne.

Before every game, I always pick 'my' team. This is the first time this season the manager has picked the same team as me!

For about half an hour, City looked really good. After 7 minutes, we nearly scored when, from Noone's free-kick, Caulker got above a defender at the back post, and his header almost fell to Mutch – unfortunately, Villa keeper, Brad Guzan, grabbed it just in time. Noone's delivery was notably better than a lot of Whittingham's. The downside was that Villa winger, Marc Albrighton, was causing problems down our left flank.

Noone then cut inside and cleverly fed Kenwyne, who had overlapped outside him. Villa skipper Ron Vlaar blocked it, and City had a decent penalty shout, as the ball sheared off his arm – but no go. A minute later, Zaha fed Campbell, who had made a good run behind and across the defenders. Campbell seemed to have clipped the ball past Guzan, but the keeper got a hand to it, and the slightest of deflections made it hit the far post, rather than go in.

From the rebound, City regained possession and fed Noone. He cut in and shot, beating Guzan but smashing against the crossbar. 'Howitzer!' as Hugh Johns may well have said, but the crossbar is no damned good to us at this stage of the season. I told you we had used up all our luck in the Norwich game.

City continued to press, there was lots of movement, but no more clear-cut chances. After half an hour, Mutch limped off and Eikrem came on. He played one good ball to Campbell, but most of the time played too deep to pose any real attacking threat. I feel the Norseman could play instead of Medel, but if we play the two together we are in danger of becoming a blunt instrument – as we are when Medel and Whitts play together.

City's goal threat gradually petered out, and in the second half, it was all Villa. Sensing a win, they gradually pushed more men forward, and in the end we were just hanging on. Zaha looked worse and worse as the game went on, constantly trying to come inside, even when it was clear that the space was on the outside. This is the problem with playing these wingers (so-called!) on their 'wrong' wings. Dæhli, the 18-year-old Scandi kid, came on and showed some nice touches, but he is no winger, he is more of a central midfielder, so there was a lack of width. Also, this kid is not great at tracking back, so he can be a liability defensively.

In stoppage time, Weimann had a chance from close range, but Marshall got a hand to it and pushed it over. So that's why they call it stoppage time!

So, we played our best team and still weren't good enough to win, playing at home against a struggling side. Conclusion: we are going down, because we aren't good enough.

End of – until the next game!

Dear Diary,
Thursday, 13 February 2014

This club never ceases to amaze me.

The enthusiastic Cardiff City fan base has pretty much got over its broken romance with Malky, only for the club to release a bizarre statement today criticising deals under Mackay's reign, such as the purchase of Andreas Cornelius for £10 million. The Great Dane has been sold by Ole, of course, and the statement – issued by Chief Executive Simon Lim – describes how the club has incurred a loss in excess of £8.5 million on the deal. Lim explains how 'key shareholders' have made their dissatisfaction at such a huge loss known to the board, believing the original purchase to be due to 'imprudent and careless management undertaken by the previous football management'.

I mean, what is the point of that, eh??

Dear Diary,
Friday, 14 February 2014

Blimey, now even Ole is at it!

OGS has come out today, moaning how the funds available to him are nowhere near the amount of cash that Tan stuck in Malky's Valentine's card back in the day.

Talk about getting your excuses in early, eh?

Dear Diary,
Saturday, 15 February 2014

Cardiff City 1 – 2 Wigan Athletic

FA Cup

k/o 3.00 p.m.

Okay, we are going down. I have accepted it. I accepted it ages ago, after the Palace away game actually, which was back at the start of November. (Check my match report if you don't believe me!)

I had a brief notion that maybe things would change under Ole, but alas, the players he has brought in do not look good enough to make any difference. So back to the Championship it is.

If we are going down, then can we at least do something worthwhile as we go down? Like maybe, win the FA Cup? After all, Wigan performed this feat for the first time last season. They are now a Championship club, and we only have to beat them – at home – to reach the last eight. Then we are only two games from Wembley. (Actually, we are then only one game from Wembley, since they adopted the bad practice of having semi-finals there as well – but you know what I mean.) Another thing is, we could qualify for the Europa League next season, as we are top of the 'Fair Play League'. But thinking about things like that is just silly.

Okay, so we have Wigan at home, in the FA Cup 5th round. There are lots of new players, and Ole needs to get them used to playing together. So we keep to our strongest side, right? Wrong. He makes a raft of changes, with the new Spanish signing, Cala, coming into an ever-changing defence, which now boasts Andrew Taylor back at left-back. The Norwegian trio of Eikrem, Dæhli and Berget all start. Even 'Malky's lovechild', Don Cowie, makes a return to the match-day squad, albeit on the bench. But, of course, he comes on (why?).

The result of all these changes? City lose 2–1 at home to a Championship side, and the brief 'dream' of achieving a relegation and FA Cup 'double' goes out the window.

Oh, did I mention that we could get into the Europa League next season if we win the Fair Play League … ?

Dear Diary,

Wednesday, 19 February 2014

I know that it's fun to speculate, but, have you seen the *Echo* today? Wilf Zaha worth a place on the World Cup plane to Rio?
Really???

I must have been watching the wrong bloke.

Dear Diary,

Friday, 21 February 2014

Gareth – we have another of those 'must-win' games you enjoy so much tomorrow. Can we do it?

No. I gave up hope weeks ago, remember?

I reckon it will be a draw. 1–1. Is there such a thing as a 'must-draw' game???

I have no idea, Dave. Really I don't.

Dear Diary,

Saturday, 22 February 2014

Cardiff City 0 – 4 Hull City

k/o 3.00 p.m.

Not a good day for City fans, this.

Ole put out another strange-looking team, with loads of changes from the last League game: Fabio, already discarded once (and subbed twice), mysteriously back in the ever rotating right-back role, Cala in central defence for Turner (our best defender recently), the already discarded Taylor back in at left-back for Declan John. So three of the back four have been changed – not usually a great idea.

In midfield, Ole has problems, as Medel (who has been good lately) and Mutch are both out. Surely Whitts will now come back in? But no, Ole has a better plan, and Eikrem is paired in the midfield with Don Cowie. Curiouser and curiouser ...

I looked at the side before the game, displayed as it was on my mate's phone, and predicted we would lose 3–0. How wrong I was! We were even worse than that, and lost 4–0 – to a side who finished below us in the Championship last season, lest we forget.

City had some chances: Zaha weaved inside and hit a strong shot which Allan MacGregor saved; there were crucial blocks by Hull defenders on Eikrem and Kenwyne; there were some strong penalty shouts, which Howard Webb studiously ignored. (We have still not been awarded a penalty all season; mind you, we haven't conceded one either.) But we could not score.

Hull broke forward about four times, and scored on every occasion. We are terribly weak in both penalty areas, the usual mark of a relegation side.

We have now gone from losing games by the odd goal, to losing them by 3 or 4 goals. Ole, who has been here for eight weeks and ten games, has no idea what his best side is. If he cannot judge the relative abilities of players, then what is he doing being a manager? He is just pretending!

What have we learned from this? City are going down, not with a bang but a whimper. We may not win another game all season, and we are bloody lucky to have won the five we have. Unless Ole gets a grip soon, City will have to get rid of him. If he is still this clueless at the start of next season, then we will be swiftly found out in the Championship, and could be facing another relegation battle.

What are the positives? Hull have a good set of fans. They sang a song based on 'Cum On Feel the Noize', and had us all clapping them for chanting, 'Stand Up for Your History', which created a communion between us and them. (We both have foreign owners who want to change kits, team names and things.) This is unusual at football games, where fans are usually trying to emphasise the difference between teams. (I even spotted a Bluebirds CCFC banner at the back of the away end, complete with 'old' badge, Gareth.)

And it was a nice day today: no wind, no rain, and quite mild. Maybe spring is on the way.

Oh, and Zaha got booked, but that was our only 'yellow'. So we are still doing well in the Fair Play League ...

Dear Diary,

Sunday, 23 February 2014

Social media is not everyone's cup of tea. I realise that.

But look at this message below posted yesterday by Bluebirds Unite. It's an emotional response to the sorry state in which we now find ourselves:

You've had your fun,
Your experiments haven't worked. Please stop your nonsense before it's too late and there is no Cardiff City left.
Best thing to happen to Cardiff City?
Not bloody likely – Red & Dead!!!
Well done.

For me, this sums up the whole sorry debacle. We knew this was likely to be a tough season, but we are cutting our own throats here. One league win under Tan's new manager; no shape to our defence, tonked by Swansea and continued unrest over the rebranding.

'You took my dreams and made them your own. You had no right to do that, for the dreams were mine, not yours.'

Happy Birthday, Mr Tan.

		P	W	D	L	F	A	Diff	Pts
	WBA	27	4	13	16	31	39	−8	25
18	Sunderland	26	6	6	14	26	42	−16	24
19	Cardiff City	27	5	7	15	19	48	−29	22
20	Fulham	27	6	3	18	27	59	−32	21

Dear Diary,

Monday, 24 February 2014

You know that thing you do when the kids are misbehaving in the back of the car? You know, you half turn around and yell 'If you two don't ruddy well behave we are NOT taking you on holiday this year!'

Well, OGS has only gone and followed up that threat. Clearly he had enough of his eleven badly behaved kids after last Saturday's debacle, and has pulled the plug on this week's family holiday to Dubai. Instead, the brats will stay at home, revising in the cold and damp ahead of Sunday's exam up in Tottenham.

Dear Diary,

Tuesday, 25 February 2014

Oh, there is more! Now the club have taken great steps to assure us that the decision to cancel that Dubai trip really was the sole decision of the manager, and in no way was there any influence from on high. No way, for example, was a 'crisis meeting' called by the chairman after the game.

Now as if we'd ever have thought that, eh?

Dear Diary,

Thursday, 27 February 2014

I know we need little help from others in making life difficult, but sometimes it feels as if the whole world is against us.

Today, for example, we discover that our fixture later this year away to Sunderland has been switched to ... Sunday 26 April at 12 noon. Thus, those of us planning on making this estimated 316 mile, 11½ hour round trip, face a 3.30 a.m. departure and probably work or school or college the next day.

Fair play to our old pal Tony Jefferies of TIT tours, mind. He has thrown together an overnight trip departing on the Saturday for only £70.

(You're doing that one on your own, Dave ...)

Eight

BEWARE,
THE IDES OF MARCH

Dear Diary,

Saturday, 1 March 2014

Dydd Gŵyl Dewi

Before Shakespeare's time, the 'Ides of March' didn't carry any particular significance, you know. The notion of the Ides (which is actually 15 March – Everton away) being a date to fear was purely the Bard's invention because it fitted a view of history that he was trying to create. It was simply his take on how the soothsayer warned Caesar of his impending doom. Old Will would have had a field day with Vincent Tan's spin on history and culture, wouldn't he?

The high-trousered one was in his element himself today, rewriting history on *Football Focus*. Tan waxed lyrical on how Dave Jones was better than Malky; how he was the saviour of our club; how the Anti-red brigade were only a 'few hundred people' and much else beside. The owner even suggested that City fans owed him an apology for all the shit that had come his way.

The interview was first broadcast on the World Service in the early hours of yesterday morning, in fact, so by the time *FF* began at midday, message boards, social media sites and the local press were full of Tan's contemplations. With no actual game to distract us today, there was little else to do but follow the reaction to what Tan had to say. The *South Wales Echo* carried the story over eight pages, for instance.

Do you know, this diary should be a colourful description of a memorable, exciting season, but it is slowly becoming the definitive textbook on the art of self-destruction.

Dear Diary,

Sunday, 2 March 2014

Spurs 1 – 0 Cardiff City

k/o 4.00 p.m.

We changed our formation for this one, Ole going for a sweeper system marshalled by the Spaniard, Juan Cala, with Caulker and Turner playing in front of him. It almost worked, as we frustrated Spurs for a long time – but alas, we still went down to another defeat, and of course 'almost' does not get you any points, in this or any other league.

For once Marshall did not have to make loads of amazing saves. We actually restricted Spurs to only a handful of chances or half chances. For all that, though, the goal, conceded just after the half-hour mark, was somewhat preposterous.

We have, effectively, three central defenders, the idea being that we thwart Spurs' attacking intentions. But what happens when we have a corner or an attacking free-kick? We send all three of them up for it, of course! This would be fine if we knew how to defend a counter-attack – but we don't. We got caught out by a sucker punch from our own corner at Liverpool, and the same thing happened here.

From the clearance, Spurs broke down our right with Andros Townsend, who made ground before feeding Adebayor. He put a low cross towards Soldado, who was the only attacker in our penalty area. We had three defenders in the box, running back, but none of them had taken the decision to get tight to Soldado, who had an easy tap-in to score. As seemed to happen quite a lot early on in the campaign, Medel – supposedly our defensive midfielder – was the closest man to Soldado, but was not close enough. Medel seems to think his role involves running back and 'defending a zone'. He doesn't seem to think it entails retreating and then 'marking a player'. Maybe one of our coaches should tell him!

City had one real chance to score. Predictably this was from a set piece, Caulker getting up above their defence and smacking a header against the bar. It was probably easier to score than to miss, but there you go. There was also a half chance when Declan John overlapped down the left and smashed in a shot, which Spurs' keeper, Lloris, parried at the near post. Bellamy had managed to get into the box, and was screaming for a cut back. Would the ball have got to Bellers if Declan had attempted the pass? Would Bellers have knocked it into the net? Who knows? On the whole, I think Declan was justified in shooting. We probably haven't shot enough this season – there has been too much 'passing the buck'. At least the youngster forced the keeper to make a save.

I should also mention Marshall, who is now looking impressive, even when he doesn't have to do much. On one occasion, a Spurs player shot from long range, and instead of parrying the ball, he caught it with both hands with supreme nonchalance, *as if it was no harder than swatting a fly. In truth, though, in many games he is our only player who looks good enough to be in this division.*

Although we expected little from this game, it's now only one win in eight League outings under Ole, which is worrying. What was worse, we got two bookings here (Bellers and Kimbo), which seriously buggers up our chances in the Fair Play League!

Dear Diary,

Monday, 3 March 2014

I decided that I would take a break tonight from the complications of the PL, with its managers who head-butt opponents; eccentric Malaysian chairmen who give pre-match dressing room pep talks stood on chairs, and wild dreams of five wins to avoid relegation, and decide to tune in to watch Chesterfield v. Portsmouth on the local pub's Sky TV.

And before you ask, yes, THAT Portsmouth, the ones who triumphed over us in the 2008 Cup Final. In a 4th Division game on a Monday night away to Chesterfield, Pompey played in .... blue and white. Expensive things, principles.

Anyway, I spotted a neat logo at one point during this TV coverage. Did you? 'FL72.' Any ideas?
Tell you tomorrow.

Dear Diary,

Tuesday, 4 March 2014

Another day, another headline. This time Tan has made the *Daily Mail.*

Apparently, in that 'pep talk' before the Spurs game, Tan offered the players a £3.7 million bonus if they stayed up, only to withdraw it once he realised that it contravened Premier League rules. He told them to shoot more too, by the way.

Anyway, did you work out that FL72 tag then? Well, there are seventy-two teams in the Football League, see, so it's 'Football League 72.'

Presumably this is the league's way of demonstrating that the Chesterfields, Portsmouths and Newport Cewntys are just as much part of the family as your Leedses, Derbys and Forests.

Not that that interests us, of course. Yet.

Dear Diary,

Wednesday, 5 March 2014

Ash Wednesday, the first day of Lent.
Wonder what Tan will give up?
If only ...

Dear Diary,

Thursday, 6 March 2014

Well, did u see him? The Bale guy last night. Awesome. Much needed, if temporary, relief in this tortuous season.

(Why did Wales wear white, Dave?)

Now if we could only superimpose this on to a City contract ...

Dear Diary,

Saturday, 8 March 2014

Cardiff City 3 – 1 Fulham

k/o 3.00 p.m.

Okay, forget all my previous reservations about calling matches 'must-win games'. If you look at the table, you can see that City are (relatively speaking) quite bad. Fulham, at rock bottom, are the only team that are even worse. This really is a 'must-win game'.

City abandon the ultra-defensive sweeper system adopted at Spurs, and go for 4-4-2, with Kenwyne Jones joining Campbell up front, and Craig Noone (injured for the Spurs game) back on the right wing. Out of the side go Cala and Gunnarsson.

Campbell makes his usual busy start, and gets in a good block on the Fulham right-back, Riether, just as he is trying to clear the ball. Result: a tremendous effort by Campbell (which will knacker him out later in the game), for the sake of which we have forced a throw-in (their throw-in, mind you, not ours) near the halfway line. Wow! This sort of thing has them raving about Fraizer in the Echo *and on* Radio Wales. *We used to have a guy who did this kind of thing twenty years ago, Carl Dale, and I really liked him as a player. But Dale used to score a few goals as well ...*

After 15 minutes, I start to get worried. Medel has managed to cut out a lot of the errors that littered his game in the early part of the season, but now he is reviving them. He gives the ball away on the edge of the box. Luckily Fulham have a Greek debutant and an unknown teenager up front, and look toothless. Marshall saves.

Then Campbell gets the ball on the edge of their box and, with twinkling toes, he beats a couple of players and fires in a shot which the keeper has to parry. Maybe I was wrong about the boy!

As we near half-time, City start to look seriously menacing. Noone puts in an early cross, Kenwyne manages to pull away from his marker and fires in a shot, which the keeper saves. Then we get a corner. The ball is headed out, then played back in to Noone, unusually hanging about on the left flank (as this is the side he took the corner from). This time Noone goes outside his man and fires in a low cross-shot which bounces off two Fulham defenders and into the legs of Caulker, who manages to bundle it over the line: 1–0 City.

A couple of minutes into the second half, Noone cuts inside from his usual berth on the right and delivers a precise cross to Kenwyne, who has again managed to peel away from his marker and is lurking at the back post. But just as we expected the ball to hit the back of the net, Kenwyne delivers a pathetically weak header which goes feebly wide.

Inevitably, we pay for this a dozen minutes later, when Fulham equalise. From a Fulham corner, Heitinga gets in the first header, and the ball lands for Lewis Holtby, probably Fulham's most dangerous attacker, who is standing completely unmarked in the middle of our 6-yard box. He knocks it in for 1–1. Whoever said that City were 'cute' defensively?!

However, the stalemate did not last long. After 67 minutes, from yet another corner, Caulker was unmarked – well, why would you bother, he's already scored from one corner, why worry about him? – and rose up to nod the ball goalwards. Even then, it looked like an easy save for Stekelenburg, the Fulham goalie. However, seemingly the header was so weak that it fooled him. He dived too soon, and the ball bounced in front of him, and then over his body as he hit the deck. It sort of trickled over the line for 2–1 City.

Four minutes later, City sealed the game with another goal which owed a lot to luck. The common factor in all of them was Noone, who again put in a cross, which this time Campbell tried to get on the end of. This time the header was saved by Stekelenburg, but he could only push the ball back out in front of him. The parry hit Riether, and rebounded off him straight into the back of the net. Comical or tragic, depending on your point of view!

City, having got into a winning position, did their best to 'make a meal' of it. They decided not to mark Holtby again, at another corner – well, why would you, etc? – but this time, Marshall saved the effort. As Fulham were not capable of getting back to 3-2, they were therefore not capable of putting us under pressure in the last couple of minutes and forcing an equaliser, which would otherwise doubtless have happened. So the final whistle blew, and City – and Ole – had finally managed to win another game. Oh, I should have said City and Tan, who came onto the pitch at the end (with the former long-serving political leader of Malaysia, Mahathir Mohammed) to receive the plaudits that were his undoubted due. Cue loads of booing!

So City have won another game. Does this mean we can win a few more, which we will need to do to stay up? No, it just means we can beat Fulham, who are rubbish. Even their own fans know they are rubbish. They told us, 'You're going down with the Fulham ...' and after this altogether unconvincing win, I fear they may well be right.

NB: Interesting to see that Robbie Fowler was one of the guest pundits on tonight's Match of the Day. No mention from anyone, in the review of this game, that the guy had ever had anything to do with City. Still, I suppose it's best forgotten ...

Dear Diary,
Thursday, 13 March 2014

I spotted an interesting titbit on the Cardiff City online message board today.

A poster calling himself (or maybe herself, I guess) 'Doctor Evil' claimed to have been in the ticket office at the CCS to renew their season ticket and was told that the ST sales were 'approaching 17,000'.

Really????

Dear Diary,
Friday, 14 March 2014

Memo to self: Do not start drinking at 8.00 a.m. again tomorrow ...

Dear Diary,

Saturday, 15 March 2014

Everton 2 – 1 Cardiff City

k/o 3.00 p.m.

It's funny, we were in the pub before this game, and I could see the back of a football stadium sticking out into the side street. 'Oh, I didn't realise we were so close to the ground,' I remarked. Only it turned out that the ground wasn't Goodison Park; it was Anfield.

You could actually see one ground, across Stanley Park, from the other, and there is only about a fifteen-minute walk between them. Funny, that. (And a little-known fact – little known outside Scouseland, that is – is that Everton originally played at Anfield; Liverpool only moved in after they moved out.)

Okay, on with the match report. Everyone thought City were unlucky after this game. Why?

Yes, we held Everton until the last minute of injury time, when they scored their winner with a mis-hit shot. Yes, for a long time we kept possession and kept them quiet, so that, at times, it appeared that they were playing on the counter-attack. Yes, we had a decent penalty shout in the closing minutes, when Zaha went down with the score at 1–1. Yes, yes, yes, but no – as at Spurs, we didn't get anything out of the game.

So, were we unlucky? No. Marshall had to pull off about three world-class saves to keep us in it. We scored with virtually our only chance of the game. For the penalty shout, Zaha went down amidst a forest of legs, having lost control of the ball and then run straight into a bunch of defenders. It looked like a stonewall penalty from where we were standing in the away section at Goodison; but on Match of the Day, *you realised it really wasn't.*

More importantly, though, why is Marshall having to save so many shots? That one is easy to explain. With the much maligned Ben Turner out injured, we now have two centre-backs: Caulker (whom England are apparently considering for the World Cup!) and Cala, who cannot tackle. They may look composed on the ball (which Turner isn't, as we well know), but they consistently back off instead of making a decisive physical challenge, hence all the shots we conceded here. With Turner alongside Caulker, sometimes his defensive weakness is not apparent, but with Cala alongside him, it is very obvious. These two guys need to learn how to defend.

To summarise: it was goalless at the interval. Everton took the lead on 59 minutes when Medel decided not to challenge Deulofeu, and he cut inside. (Why does Medel so often decide not to meddle?) His shot took an unlucky deflection off Caulker, which meant that it beat Marshall at the near post – on a day when only a deflection could possibly have beaten our keeper.

Eight minutes later, City, amazingly, were level. Kim won a dodgy free-kick on the edge of their box and, for some reason, Everton decided not to mark properly. Cala ran in between two defenders to meet Whittingham's free-kick (Whitts had come on for the injured Mutch, by the way), and bundled the ball in from close range. A probable assist with his hand was not spotted. So, after hardly creating anything, City were back to 1–1.

The score remained like this until 15 minutes from the end, when Ole gambled and put on Zaha for Fabio, who had strangely spent most of the game playing in midfield, after City quickly abandoned their sweeper system (because with Everton playing a lone striker, there was hardly anybody to mark!). This was a good move, because with Everton pushing for a winner, we could put Zaha on the halfway line, and perhaps hit them on the counter-attack.

Zaha did have a couple of chances to hit them, but on the first occasion he got confused with all his step overs and was unable to beat the lone defender he was up against. Hopeless! On the second occasion, he tried to dribble past three players – completely impossible, but he might have, on a luckier day, ended up getting a soft penalty decision. But he didn't, and to be honest, he is not really very good. But you never know – if he keeps running at people, we might get something somewhere along the line.

Then, the penalty claim having come and gone, Everton hit us with the inevitable knock-out punch. After sustained pressure at the end of the game, a cross was looped over to the far post. Gareth Barry managed to nod it back to Coleman, who was lurking (unmarked) in the 6-yard box. His mis-hit *shot beat Marshall, who had dived too soon, and sort of sliced into the net in slow motion. Okay, so I was wrong. It was a day when only a deflection or a mis-hit could have beaten our keeper – and he had the misfortune for both to happen.*

One good point: Dæhli came on as a sub and played some incisive balls forward, trying to get men moving into space. This kid could turn out to be good, but will he turn out to be good this season?

Dear Diary,

Wednesday, 19 March 2014

I must admit, life away from the diary has been a bit hectic recently, and it's actually quite late on Thursday evening when I am writing this bit so it's a bit of a composite 'catch-up' entry, to be honest.

It all seems on for the 'Big Protest March' this weekend, anyway. Lots of flyers etc. have been doing the rounds telling us the plans. We are asked to gather between 1.00 p.m. and 2.00 p.m. at the Admiral Napier pub in Cowbridge Road East, before setting off for the CCS on a 'peaceful and positive march'.

Mind you, a recent survey undertaken by the Supporters' Trust revealed this week that 85 per cent of members now want the trust to campaign against the rebrand. I am not sure the Admiral Napier is big enough to house everyone, is it?

Dear Diary,

Friday, 21 March 2014

Interesting couple of transfer snippets today – Darcy Blake has joined Newport County for the rest of the season and Earnie has gone to Blackpool!

They feel like names from my childhood.

Dear Diary,

Saturday, 22 March 2014 (1)

Lots going on both on and off the pitch today. So we have split shifts to squash it all in. Gareth will cover the match with Liverpool, and I was sent along with my notebook and pencil to cover the protest march.

Critical analysis of this event is almost impossible. Flags and banners snaked their way through Canton and along Sloper Road, in scenes reminiscent of the Jarrow March. Estimated numbers ranged from 2,500 to nearer 5,000, with many more joining the festivities in the stadium itself during the game. The march formed a meandering river of blue, led by parade marshal Annis Abraham (complete with retro 1975 blue t-shirt, blue gloves and a megaphone).

I also spotted various representatives of Cardiff City Supporters' Club, Cardiff City Supporters Trust, the Cardiff City Phone-in, CCMB and various media types with microphones and cameras. A flare was lit as we left the Admiral Napier pub. Trust members sold blue ponchos as rain threatened.

By and large, the organisers' plea for order was fairly well respected. Lots of noisy shouting, of course, and a moment when I thought that the march would storm its way into the

main reception, but on the whole, things remained calm. Billy the Badge had a field day selling his blue retro scarves.

Whether this makes any impact on Mr Tan remains to be seen. The sea of blue within the stadium on 19 minutes 27 seconds may have brought the hairs on Jason Perry's neck to life, but the reaction of the majority shareholder was to defiantly open – and later remove – his jacket, to reveal that bloody red shirt.

We may have won the battle today, but the end of the war still seems a long way off.

Dear Diary,

Saturday, 22 March 2014 (2)

Cardiff City 3 – 6 Liverpool

k/o 3.00 p.m.

A very strange score indeed for a Premier League fixture. I suppose you could argue that City, to their credit, took the game to Liverpool and twice took the lead, before eventually being taken apart.

City kept their sweeper system but made one change from Goodison. Craig Noone was injured, but Craig Bellamy was this time fit, so one Craig replaced the other in the line-up, Bellers playing in 'the hole' behind Fraizer Campbell.

City looked good early on, Theo firing over from a corner when, with greater composure, he might have scored. Then, after 9 minutes, we did take the lead. Fabio lost the ball some-where near the corner flag, but Campbell's constant harassing of defenders this time paid off. He won the ball back and saw Mutch steaming into the area. Campbell calmly cut the ball back to Mutch, who cut inside one defender and passed the ball into the net with his left foot: 1-0 City.

Liverpool scored with what seemed like their first real attack. They kept the ball in midfield for ages before shipping it out to Glen Johnson, who seemed to be in acres of space on their right. He fired in a low cross, City defenders seemed to have 'stepped up' to get players offside, and left Suarez and

Sturridge standing on their own in the 6-yard box. The ball came to Suarez and he tapped it in. A very odd-looking goal indeed; there was not even any claim for offside from the City players. 1-1 after 16 minutes, and worrying that Liverpool could score so easily.

Never mind about defence, we will simply outscore them! After 25 minutes, Mutch was again in an advanced position, where we know he can be dangerous. This time he found Campbell running through the inside right channel, with nobody tracking his run. Agger came across but Campbell cut inside him easily (as Mutch had done for the first goal), and like Mutch, he knocked it inside the far post with his left foot: 2-1 City.

Maybe we would hold out until half-time, and the second half would be tighter. Could this be a famous victory, like the Man. City game (how long ago that seems!) ... but no, after 41 minutes, Liverpool won a corner. It was half cleared, then crossed back in, and Skrtel, who we know can be a menace in these situations, showed much greater desire to get to the ball than Cala, getting in front of the Spaniard to volley the ball home from close range: 2-2 at the interval.

It was all over within 15 minutes of the restart. City met with a series of injustices when Sturridge flopped over and was awarded a free-kick on the edge of the box. From the kick, Theo was bowled over by a thunderous shot, and had to leave the field for treatment, then Mutch also had to go off. With both off the field and not allowed to return, Liverpool took their corner – and Skrtel scored again. This time he showed a little bit of movement, which left Caulker completely flat-footed. Caulker made what appeared to be a token attempt to get back to him but really got nowhere near him, and as the cross came in, Skrtel flicked a header past Marshall and into the net. So, 3-2 Liverpool, and their fans start telling us they are 'gonna win the League'.

A few minutes later, Johnson overlapped again, and pulled back a low cross. Theo was in the right position to cut it out, but the ball got caught in his legs and Sturridge reacted quickly to back heel the ball across the goal. It fell exactly to where Suarez was running, and he simply knocked it into the centre of the goal: 4-2 'pool, and game over.

There was an element of injustice to the 5th goal (as if, by then, it mattered). We attacked Johnson, and could have had a foul, but it wasn't given. Johnson hoisted a long ball towards Sturridge, which Caulker, with his greater height, was able to deal with. However, his header was weak – it didn't even reach touch – and he reacted really slowly, not doing anywhere near enough to close Sturridge down. Result: Sturridge, seeing Suarez charging towards the area, knocked the ball past the statuesque Caulker and into the path of the Uruguayan, who knocked it into an empty net. I should also have mentioned that Suarez steamed past Cala, who was yards in front of him, but seemed to be strolling back: 5-2 'pool.

City, at this point, gained a consolation goal when Theo and Zaha linked up on the right. Zaha made a decent run off the ball to take a defender away, allowing Theo space to cross the ball. Substitute Kenwyne Jones was on the end of it, and he placed an unselfish cushioned header perfectly into the path of Mutch, who waited for it to bounce, and then nodded it into the net: 5-3.

Liverpool had the last goal (the one that really counts!) after another 'vanilla' challenge from one of our two floppy centre-backs. This time it was Cala who was the culprit, allowing another long ball to bounce before trying to clear it. Result: he was shoved off the ball by Suarez (about half his size), and was left sprawling on the turf as the South American strolled up to Marshall and rolled the ball past him.

City created some decent chances, but the defending will have to be a lot better if we are to get anything in the crunch game at West Brom. We badly need Ben Turner back. We cannot stay up if we have two centre-backs who cannot make decent challenges. And England must really be in a bad way if they are seriously considering Steven Caulker for their World Cup squad!

NB: Two strange facts – prior to this game, City had beaten Liverpool in their last five home games against them (going back to the 1950s and early '60s, of course). And the last top-flight game to finish 6-3 was Man. Utd v. Oldham on Boxing Day, 1991 (so the turkey was to blame). There has never been that score before in the history of the Premier League.

Dear Diary,

Sunday, 23 March 2014

The march is all over Facebook and message boards today, and even made Sky News. Front page of *Wales on Sunday* too.

March organisers did not meet with the club chairman after the event, though. All the groups involved with organising things yesterday felt that the ten-minute slot that was offered prior to the game was insufficient time to properly discuss matters, apparently. The club seem to have acknowledged that and so we look forward to a meeting shortly.

Darcy done well for Cewnty by the way, according to *WOS*. Shored things up at the back in keeping a clean sheet at Torquay. Fancy him returning to us next season in the Championship?

Dear Diary,

Wednesday, 26 March 2014

No midweek game for City (again) so it has been a nervous few nights near a radio or huddled over my new toy, the BBC Sport website, following the kick-by-kick antics of our relegation rivals, several of whom have fixtures this week.

Sadly a last-minute equaliser at the Emirates means that Swansea City probably no longer come into that category, despite only one win under Monk all season. Our conquerors from the weekend edged past Sunderland at Anfield to strike off a game in hand for the Black Cats, though, so there was some joy for us. West Ham now seem out of it by virtue of a victory over Hull, who I reckon should still be safe anyhow.

City now have seven games left to save themselves. Popular opinion suggests that we need to beat West Brom. on Saturday, Palace the week after, Stoke, and maybe even Newcastle. Chelsea at home on the last day of the season could be the game when the 'Special One' clinches the title, which would be just our luck.

Back-to-back victories (at the Hawthorns and against Palace) would be a first for the season but there seems to be a degree of, well, maybe not confidence exactly but perhaps at least 'optimism' after recent encouraging displays. We even had a goal from a striker last week, remember! Norwich have a nightmare run-in as, like many others fighting the drop, they play a number of the big sides between now and Super Sunday.

Dave, I don't know why you put yourself through all this, really I don't. We ARE going down.

Gareth, it's a Wednesday evening and I haven't got Sky. What else would I do???

Dear Diary,

Thursday, 27 March 2014

As a member of the Supporters' Trust, I have been given an opportunity to nominate my 'Clubman of the Year.'

I have gone for Sian Branson.

That'll put the cat amongst the pigeons.

Dear Diary,

Friday, 28 March 2014

So, if Caulker is good enough to be linked with a move back to Spurs today, why are we conceding 6 goals in a home game??

Dear Diary,

Saturday, 29 March 2014

West Bromwich Albion 3 – 3 Cardiff City

k/o 3.00 p.m.

We decided to take a break from travelling all over the country this week, and once again spent the afternoon at the very welcoming Sports Bar, in the depths of Canton. What an enjoyable venue this is.

We have also decided, just for a change, to adopt a slightly different approach to today's match report. For today, we propose to bring you all the news, as it happens. Yes, we will scribble and type in real time in this crowded tavern. A bit ambitious given the number of fans around me, but here goes. For one night only … Cardiff City, LIVE. Hang on to your hats …

Right lads … predictions?

Big Andy goes for 2–0 to City, so do I.

I want to wait to see the line-up, in case Turner plays. If Turner plays: 2-1 Baggies. And if he doesn't, 4-1 Baggies.

We arrive seconds before kick-off. Three or four deep at the bar. Giant screens are surrounded by City fans of all ages. The commentator talks excitedly of fans needing to play their part. The Sports Bar is ready to do its bit.

Less than 2 minutes in … and the predictions dive down the drain as Morgan Amalfitano lobs Marshall to give WBA the lead. Nervous defending follows. We have barely started our pints and the game is already a car crash.

If they score another it's all over.

Andy is already planning an away match at Blackburn. Marshall makes his customary one-handed wonder-save. Despite the offside.

'Coaches hate avoidable goals,' says the bloody commentator.

9 minutes … The Baggies f**kin' score again! We don't seem to have even touched the ball yet.

Huge applause next, for Jeff Astle, around the stadium for some reason.

I didn't even know he was playing?

We have a sweeper system, no creative players and we are 2 down after 10 minutes.

14 minutes have now passed in the blink of an eye. I don't think their keeper has touched the ball yet. We move to a different screen in search of a better view, and better luck. OGS looks like his mother has just died.

After 17 minutes, in a rare moment of calm, we decide that Marshall was not at fault for that well-taken first goal. Poor header from Medel though.

18 minutes … a first touch for Bellamy.

City get a cross in as, at last, we start to settle. We are hoping that WBA think the hard work is all done. Blimey, we have a corner now. And another. Oh, no, apparently not. I am balancing the iPad on my knee.

We are actually controlling the game now, if it wasn't 2-0 down we'd be quite happy.

Albion respond with a corner and a run of five crosses, as we fail to close people down with gay abandon.

30 minutes – Jordan Mutch lobs the keeper in almost a replica of the first goal!

He won't be with us next season.

City have the bit between their teeth now.

We can win this!

City fans at the Hawthorns are in fine voice, we can hear them in here in Canton. The whole pub joins in the singing. 'Blue Army!!!'

34 minutes ... Zaha gets stripped. A passing MILF distracts me momentarily as Gunnars takes an almighty clout. Zaha on for Fabio. Are we going 4-4-2?

36 minutes ... Baggies goalie, Ben Foster, resorts to time wasting. After 36 minutes??? Medel shoots wide as half-time looms. I would almost take this score at HT.

Campbell is almost through ... it's hectic stuff. He is being penalised every couple of moments. 4 minutes of added time. At last we reach that 49th minute. (F**k me, this is hard work.)

The half-time TV graphics confirm, via a complex series of pie charts and histograms, that City are losing 2-1. Palace are drawing with Chelsea. Rumours spread that Ledley is up front with Cameron Jerome. The Jacks are beating Norwich. Academic if we get beat, declares Simon the Sage, who has now joined the throng.

The game restarts. Back to the one-legged typing ... Pressure from Baggies ... but we stand tall. Dæhli is on. No idea who has gone off. Gareth is sat on the pool table now, his ball is over the centre pocket.

A shot from Volumbu *(is that how you spell it??? [Mulumbu])* is deflected nervously wide. This ruddy commentator reminds us that City don't want to concede a 3rd goal. No shit, Sherlock!

Aaagh ... the Baggies are clean through after shoddy play but ... it's lumped over the bar.

We are not really in this in the second half.

Bellers forces a corner. (I mean a throw.) Zaha goes down in the box and wants a penalty. See Everton away. Free-kick now.

We can score from this.

But we don't.

But it's all City now. A passage of end-to-end play follows. It's all very loose, though it's totally gripping. Zaha loses possession again. And again.

There is no end product to him.

Gareth heads for the bar. Bellamy is looking knackered. Home fans are edgy in their seats. I grab the seat on the pool table, trying desperately to think up a line about being snookered if we lose this one. Marshall does a spot of eye-watering keepy uppy to chip the ball over the striker's head. F**k.

Good football sees City in the box as that nightmare start seems like a different game. We crave an equaliser, even though 2–2 doesn't really help us in terms of a result.

73 minutes ... Caulker!!!!!!! Yes ... a looping header. Bedlam in the pub. 'The blues are staying up,' we sing lustily. Curses from a guy who missed the goal while in the toilet. And a wanker of a City fan in front of me will get f**king planted if he don't keep still.

Ole's mum has been raised from the dead by the look of him now. Bellamy goes down with a knock.

They are playing like they think they can win!

It's 5 goals in the last two games, 3 for Mutch. Caulker is almost our top scorer. A display of blue scarves is held aloft behind the City goal. Dæhli goes close as City go for the win ...

Fouls all over the pitch now as French Kev goes down next. Is Jones coming on? I miss that bit, thanks to the MILF again. GB makes a dash for a slash. Medel goes down, buying him precious extra seconds.

Dæhli is down now. I can't keep up with this ... Jones never actually came on. Weird. Whitts is coming on now. Amazingly, we are in the 86th minute. Medel is off for Whitts and does the Ayatollah as he departs the field.

88 minutes now. Bloody hell ...

4 minutes of added time are signalled.

We need a winner, Dave. (Yes, I bloody know!!!!)

End to end fouling as both teams chase a 3rd. It feels like we have played half an hour of added time as a City attack comes to nothing. Nails being bitten to the core ...

Then the Baggies f***ing score with 1 minute to go. Through Marshall's legs. It's Everton all over again. And Spurs ... *(and Sunderland)* City have been chasing the game and left gaps at the back. Another pearl from the silver tongue of

Simon ... 'if supporting Cardiff City was easy, everyone would do it'. I hate football.

Aaaagh!!! Dæhli has bloody scored in the 5th of the 4 added minutes! Cue absolute bedlam here. He has turned neatly and hooked in a shot calmly like an old pro. The Sports Bar is total noise. I hug the fidgety wanker in front of me like a long-lost brother.

He turned on a sixpence ... just like Messi.

As Bill McLaren used to say, the referee's whistle goes, for the end of the match. We are absolutely exhausted. The iPad has amazingly avoided the beer. The managers embrace. They both know that it is not enough. The away end looks like Trafalgar Square on New Year's Eve.

Back in the Sports Bar, amidst the debris and spilt ale, Simon has the last word – 'Well, what the f**k did I just see???'

What the f**k, indeed.

Dear Diary,

Sunday, 30 March 2014

Well after that little lot yesterday, we ended the evening in the Claude and the Tandoori Mahal. I have the mother of all hangovers today. Oh yeah, Happy Mother's Day, Mum.

Just when you thought it was safe ...

Nine

APRIL
SHOWERS?

Dear Diary,

Tuesday, 1 April 2014

I feared the worst today, to be honest.

Given the histrionics and mayhem that we have encountered so far this season, a day specifically set aside for tomfoolery and shenanigans may just have been too much for fate to resist.

Thankfully though, there were no outlandish news stories about Martians landing in the Ninian Stand or spaghetti plants growing behind the goal to amuse us.

The closest we came to a football-related April Fools jape was a suggestion that Plymouth Argyle were going to paint their pitch orange, so that their green-shirted players could stand out more. I suppose they could always change their kit to a new colour, of course. But then, why would anyone do that???

Dear Diary,

Wednesday, 2 April 2014

Well, that didn't last long did it? That'll learn me for writing the diary in my lunch hour.

By the time I arrived home yesterday, message boards and social media were awash with bogus rumours and wild Photoshop images showing potential new blue kits for next year. One garish entry looked like something

David Beckham's new Miami Spice FC would wear, only in blue ... complete with bluebird.

One CCMB poster declared, 'I'd accept it in a heartbeat.'

There was even a rumour on Twitter that the stadium would be renamed 'The Dragon's Lair'. Though given the wealth of broken promises and heartache in recent years, maybe that should be 'The Dragon's Liar'.

Dear Diary,

Friday, 4 April 2014

Well, here we go again then. Another roller coaster of emotions lies ahead this weekend.

Will Joe Ledley do the Ayatollah? Will Danny Gabbidon play? Will Jerome celebrate when he (inevitably) scores at our end? Or will City sign Palace reserve keeper, Wayne Hennessy, to replace star man David Marshall next season?

We also ponder the situation of our relegation rivals Sunderland today, who, despite fielding an ineligible player – Ji Dong-Won – in five (yes FIVE) first team games earlier this season, face only a fine and no points deduction whatsoever. MK Dons, who were dumped out of the Capital One Cup by the Black Cats during this spell, are, not surprisingly, 'livid'.

I don't know, whatever would we talk about without football, eh?

Dear Diary,

Saturday, 5 April 2014

Cardiff City 0 – 3 Crystal Palace

k/o 3.00 p.m.

And so, we finally came to the end of the road. After this game, even the most dogged of City optimists were awoken to reality, and knew that City's adventure in the Premier League would soon be over. It is no longer a question of 'if' we are going to be relegated, but rather 'when'.

The reason that City are going down is that we have consistently been one of the poorest teams in the division. Currently, one would have to say that we are not just 'one of the poorest' teams – we are the worst, by a country mile.

It was always going to be touch and go whether or not we stayed up under Malky, because his tactics were so negative. There was a possibility of improvement under a new manager – but also a possibility of getting worse. Under Ole, the evidence is now undeniable: we have got worse. Much worse. Not only have his seven signings not made any real impact, but even the players who were doing reasonably well before Ole took over are now looking poor. Ole promised more attacking play, which we needed. Alas, not only is the defence (our strong point) now a shambles, but we look more clueless going forward than we did under Malky – some achievement indeed.

After more than three months in charge, Ole continues to reshuffle his team (and his bench) every game, as though he is still not clear who are his best players, and what is his best system. Such is the lack of ideas, and the lack of co-ordination, in both defence and attack, that you wonder what the hell they are practising in training every day. Not only is Ole no Premier League manager, he doesn't seem to be any kind of a coach, either.

City made their usual quota of three changes for this game, plus a change of formation from the sweeper system to 4-5-1. Kenwyne Jones was now back in the side as a lone striker (despite Ole not thinking it was even worth bringing him on at West Brom!), with Campbell posted on one wing, and the 'enigmatic' Zaha on the other. The other new element was young Dæhli, who after grabbing the late equaliser at the Hawthorns, was now given a crucial starting role in central midfield.

Now this Dæhli is an interesting feller-me-lad. Ole tells the press he is 'the next David Silva'. For a teenager, he is very assured; he wants the ball all the time, and is forever indicating, by hand gestures, exactly where he wants it played. The trouble is, when he has it, he often doesn't seem to do very much with it.

His style here seemed to consist of getting the ball, taking a lot of touches whilst running sideways, and then doing a little lay-off, either backwards or sideways. Then he would drift into a position further forward, trying to find a 'hole', and hope somebody else would be able to pass the ball to him in this position. The problem is that Dæhli was supposed to be our playmaker, and nobody else in the side remotely had the wit to be able to pass the ball to him in such a confined space.

There was one occasion when Dæhli could have got us something. Kenwyne Jones won a header (he put in a decent shift today, incidentally), and knocked it down for Dæhli, who was running into the box to support him. But before the young Norseman could play the ball, he was rudely bundled over from behind by a Palace defender, who clearly made no contact with the ball. Surely this was a clear penalty – but no, we don't get them, do we, and this was another one we didn't get, referee Phil Dowd waving 'play on'. Now, remember I agreed that the Zaha shout at Goodison really wasn't a penalty? Well, this one really was. *What else did the defender have to do to concede one – decapitate him?*

Alas, by this time we were already a goal down. Our marking was, again, abject. From the first Palace corner, the queerly named Dikgacoi (don't start me going on players' names again) had acres of space in which to shoot, but he ballooned the ball over the bar. Then Jason Puncheon, playing wide on the right despite being allergic to using his right foot, was allowed to switch the ball to his left and fire in a shot, which Marshall easily saved. But you can't say we hadn't been warned.

Warnings, though, mean nothing to this lot. After half an hour, Puncheon gave the ball to our old boy, Joe Ledley, on the right side of the area, and then trotted into the box. Andrew Taylor, who was supposedly marking Puncheon, took ages to notice this piece of cunning movement (i.e. jogging in a straight line into space), and by the time he became aware of it, the winger had got the ball back from Ledley. Taylor then stepped a couple of paces towards Puncheon, then stopped – standing just far away enough from him to allow Puncheon to shoot, and score. To think we dropped Declan John for Taylor, who we knew from his earlier run in the side possessed neither the ability to attack nor to defend very well. But somehow these pertinent facts appeared to escape Ole!

By half-time, it was clear that we were never going to be able to break down the well-organised Palace defence with what we had. The trouble was, what did we have on the bench? With Kenwyne and Campbell both starting, there were no more strikers to come on. (Yes, it's true: we have only two strikers at the club, since Gestede and Cornelius were sold, and Mason and Maynard allowed to go out on loan, during the transfer window. Another example of poor planning from Ole.)

We did have Eikrem, who has occasionally shown the ability to knock a decent pass forward, but curiously he was not brought on. Instead Ole introduced Noone (who wasn't fit), Bellamy (who can't run anymore) and Cowie (who runs around a lot, but rarely achieves anything). The replacement of Kenwyne for Cowie seemed to be completely random. We might as well have brought on Joe Lewis, the sub goalkeeper.

Palace inevitably increased their lead when City couldn't defend a simple set piece. Chamakh got in between defenders to get his head to it with ridiculous ease. Marshall managed a good one-handed save, but the ball came back out and hit Ledley on the knee, and went in. Ledley, to his credit, made no fuss about it at all.

The score went to 3–0 when Puncheon was again allowed to cut in on his left foot, and then unleashed a powerful shot which curled around Marshall. A very good finish, but 'Captain Fantastic' Caulker was seen once again adopting his favourite posture of 'backing off' rather than 'making a challenge'. And no effort was made by our supposed World Cup hopeful to usher Puncheon onto his useless right foot.

So we are now bereft of hope with five more games to go. How are we going to motivate ourselves for those five games? By forgetting about relegation, and focusing on the serious things. We still haven't been awarded or conceded a penalty; we need to keep this run going until the end of the season. We still haven't had a player sent off. Nobody has done any of these things in the Premier League before.

And we could still win the Fair Play League. People may scoff about this, but it's a trophy. Arsene Wenger and David Moyes would kill to win the Fair Play League right now!

Dear Diary,

Sunday, 6 April 2014

Thought I'd try something different today, so I wandered onto the Crystal Palace message board via 'holmesdale.net, the Palace Supporters Website' to see what their reaction was to yesterday's debacle, described so eloquently by my fellow diarist above.

I will spare you the not unexpected Pullis love-in threads and Joe Ledley tributes, but you may be interested in the thoughts of a poster who uses the name 'Bald Eagle' (see what he did there?).

He wrote:

> We've done the double over Cardiff and Hull! The two teams that went up automatically, spent more money than us, and we were supposed to be the worst team in premiership history? Boy do I love supporting this club through the mostly downs and ups, I'd love to finish at the end of the season above both of them and proving lots of people wrong.

Does that sound like gloating to you?

Dear Diary,

Monday, 7 April 2014

Well, the April showers are pouring down today, and I am afraid the world and his wife have the raindrops pouring down on Ole's head. The local boys gave him a right kicking, courtesy of the *Echo* etc., but the likes of Steve Claridge also got stuck in on 5 Live, criticising his lack of guile as a manager.

The Norseman *(hey that's my phrase!!)* even caught the eye of our friends at the Trinity Mirror data unit, who have taken a look at the number of changes to each Premier League starting XI between games to see which manager can justifiably be called the Premier League's biggest tinker-man. The results – calculated from games played since the turn of the year – show Ole Gunnar Solskjær is second in the list of Premier League tinker-men, having made an average of 3.25 changes to his starting XIs. David Moyes is first, by the way.

Quite how you make 0.25 of a change defeats me somewhat, though; maybe you take off a little guy like Kim or Dæhli??

Dear Diary,
Tuesday, 8 April 2014

Interesting stuff from the far north here ...

Following their recent ballot of season card holders, Hull City confirmed today that the majority of votes cast were in favour of Hull Tigers, with the Allam family continuing to lead the club. 15,033 season card holders were eligible to vote, but only 5,874 bothered to take part. Of these, only 2,565 said 'Yes' to Hull Tigers 'with the Allam family continuing to lead the club', and 2,517 said 'No' to Hull Tigers. So 792 were not too concerned, and would continue to support the club either way.

I calculate there that the 'yes' votes won by a mere 48 votes, but ... 9,159 who failed to even vote! Really?? Presumably that 9,000 care so little for their club that they won't be making the trip to Wembley this weekend for the FA Cup semi-final against Sheffield United. Hull City fans always make a decent row in support of their boys, but that's an overwhelming show of apathy, isn't it?

Would we be that uninterested, I wonder?? I like to think not, though it would be nice to be given the choice.

Dear Diary,
Wednesday, 9 April 2014

To be honest, this always looked an interesting event. And, in the light of recent results, it was looking increasingly unmissable.

But as things turned out ... well, at times, it was to border on the unprintable.

Cardiff City Supporters' Trust had somehow persuaded OGS to take part in a Q&A session tonight at the Cardiff City Stadium. It seemed to be a joint effort with the Supporters' Club, though to be honest, I spotted more people from the trust than from CCSC. Host Rob Philips led the evening, before a surprisingly sparse audience.

Rob kicked it off with a few worthy plaudits about how many managers would have cried off this evening's fixture with a niggling hamstring, in the light of recent results. But OGS had honoured the commitment so ... 'nuff respect was due: 1-0, Ole.

Bonus point to Rob Philips for tossing in the fact that OGS was missing United v. Bayern for this do and, well, nothing ever happens in that fixture, does it? (Think about it ...). Nice touch.

Ole kicked off by describing how Tan was supportive ... even after a 3-0 defeat, and answered questions about the rebranding, and his family, safely and predictably.

But that was it as far as niceties went. Rob Philips dived in, seeking explanations as to why we were so crap against Palace. Ole admitted we were 'poor', describing weak defending ... and subsequent sleepless nights. He feared the hook, but instead ... got the hug. Interesting.

Then came unprintable admission number one, about Ole's definition of the word 'loyalty'. I am going to disappoint you by observing his request to treat his revelations in confidence, and suggest you read *Ole: My Season as a PL Manager* the day it comes out. It isn't a reference to a player though ...

Despite his youth, Ole certainly reminded the audience that, actually, he and his backroom staff had more PL experience than most managers (Brendan who??) and that, eventually, he would get this right for Cardiff City. Whether 'eventually' was to arrive before 11 May was not explored.

We looked ahead to forthcoming games. We were given to understand that there would be limited changes again this year. He took questions on tinkering and his best XI – Whitts would feature.

Any talent in the wings?

Rhys Healey was a young OGS, and our loan players were getting good experience out at Bolton, Yeovil etc. Watch out for youngster Tom James too, we heard.

More unprintables followed ...

We learned who was 'pissing blood' after the Palace game. We discovered which players had been bought to be sold for more money. We had critical stuff about Danish strikers, positive stuff about Merthyr-born defenders and an eye-watering comparison of one current midfielder with

Franz Beckenbauer! Ole's definition of 'like for like' also had me pondering. (Think dreadlocks ...)

I have to say though, Ole was impressive at this event. He gave insights about how Premier League footballers prepare for big games. He disclosed intricacies that most fans would never ever know. Most importantly, he reminded everyone that, actually, he IS OGS and, ya know what? He DOES know his shit.

Whether that will be enough to save us in the next five games, well ...

I am not sure that was really the point, to be honest.

Dear Diary,

Friday, 11 April 2014

Well, there was I respecting Ole's wish to keep things under our hats from Wednesday, yet I woke today to discover that a secret I was told two days ago is now all over the TV and radio.

Some oaf on the CCFC backroom staff had revealed the team to Palace last Friday, by all accounts. Culprits are likely to be sacked, Tan is in uproar and the Palace chairman can hardly believe it.

This season just can't end quickly enough for me, I am afraid.

Dear Diary,

Saturday, 12 April 2014

Southampton 0 – 1 Cardiff City

k/o 3.00 p.m.

There was that ridiculous story going into this game, that during the week before the previous game (Palace), some-body on City's backroom staff had leaked Ole's team selection to Palace boss, Tony Pulis.

The most amazing revelation of this tale is that Ole actually selects his starting line-up during the week. I was under the impression that he just put twenty names in a hat an hour before kick-off, and drew out the first eleven ...

Now Ole had also said, at a meeting with the Supporters' Trust, that he would no longer be tinkering so much with the team – although Whittingham would be brought back, because he 'has the same composure as Beckenbauer'. This is the same Whittingham that Ole hasn't been picking for the last few weeks. Coming after Ole's assertion that Dæhli is the new David Silva, I think we can now safely state that virtually nothing our manager says is worth listening to!

The line-up for this game is another case in point. No more tinkering? He had the recently dropped Cala back in for Turner (dropped, recalled, dropped again) at centre-back. Andrew Taylor, previously brought back at left-back for the blameless Declan John, was now dropped again to make way for Fabio – whom virtually no City supporter believes should be in the side at all.

And that's just the defence! There is more. We now have Kim on the right of midfield instead of Zaha, Whittingham back in the centre of midfield for Dæhli, and Dæhli shunted out to the left, where Fraizer Campbell had started against Palace. But Campbell is okay, he is now back up front as the lone striker, instead of Kenwyne Jones. (That's six changes, by the way; from a guy who wasn't going to tinker anymore.) I thought Jones did okay against Palace, but he is now out of the side, and not even on the bench. Of course, he might be injured – but with Ole in charge of proceedings, who knows?

Okay, I think we have established that I have little faith in our manager, and hence little expectation of getting anything out of this game. City's first-half performance does nothing to change my mood. Most of the time, we can barely string three passes together or get out of our own half.

Me and my mate Andy are watching on one of these Arab TV channels, and they have a Scottish pundit who we think is Ray Houghton. He is absolutely scathing towards City – if you think I am a bit harsh at times (I think I am merely brutally realistic), then you should listen to this guy! He is amazed at how slow and pedestrian the central midfield duo of Medel and Whittingham is – 'They must be so easy to play against.' (Yet the Echo *has been raving about Medel as though he is some kind of match-winner all season ....) 'They don't actually seem to want to keep the ball,' Houghton declares at one point. It sounds like he's never seen a team as bad as us in the Premier League before!*

The only weird thing is that half-time arrives, and Southampton still haven't scored. In fact, they haven't had that many clear-cut chances, although they did hit the crossbar on one occasion, and Marshall had to make one other decent save. They have totally outplayed us, without actually creating that much. Is this down to better defensive organisation? Hmm, maybe – or maybe just luck!

'The problem is,' Andy declares, 'because it's 0-0, Ole will probably tell them they're doing well.'

'Yeah,' I agree. 'And Southampton will just up the pace a bit, and end up winning 2 or 3-0.'

The second half begins, and Southampton don't seem to be doing much at all. You still can't really see City having the wit to score a goal, though, unless – maybe a set piece. Yeah, maybe a set piece – if we can manage to get one ...

Then we get a set piece.

Southampton half clear the ball to Cala, standing on the edge of the area. He chests it down, but by the time the ball drops to his feet a defender is running towards him, so he knocks the ball to his side, to evade the challenge. This brings the ball onto his weaker left foot, and it's running away from him, too, so there is no way he will be able to fire in a decent shot. We know this. Cala shoots, the ball spins off the end of his boot, and somehow ends up in the far corner of the net: 1-0 City. Unbelievable!

Saints apply a bit more pressure, and Marshall has to make two smart saves to keep us ahead. Then we break and Zaha, on as a sub, beats two defenders – the first two defenders he has ever beaten in a City shirt – and almost scores, his shot saved by the keeper's knees. Then the final whistle blows, and we have recorded our second away win of the season. The first was at Fulham in September.

'Can we still stay up now?' Andy asks breathlessly.

No, we were just lucky. 'But now we will be more confident for the Stoke game next week.' Then Ole will make another four or seven changes, and the confidence will evaporate.

'But ... but ...'

No, don't start telling me we can avoid relegation again. Don't start trying to instil hope in me again! Hope is too painful.

But it was nice to win this game. And we are playing some poor teams in the next couple of games, too ...

Dear Diary,
Sunday, 13 April 2014

My idea, last week, of seeing what opposition fans make of us seems to have caught on. 'Appreciative Saint' today posted the following message on one of our notice boards. It's an interesting take on things:

Not all Saints fans are narrow minded.

It was not too long ago that we were annually battling relegation and didn't give a toss how we won as long as we got three points. It was also not too long ago that we were bottom of League One so most of us act with a degree of humility.

Yes it was disappointing to lose at home yesterday but for all our pretty football, we were not able to stick the bag of air in the back of the net. The performance of your keeper alone was enough for you to deserve not to lose.

Whilst most people will rave about Barca-esque styles of play, it takes a team with heart and fight to go away from home when in imminent danger of relegation, defend deep but effectively and then take a chance when it arrives. Add the passion of your support to the strength of your team and you stand a great chance of staying up – I hope you do.

Something that has gotten lost in this cash obsessed era is tradition. Whilst blue is not my favourite colour (!), that's the colour you are supposed to play in and your demonstration of that yesterday was vocal and loud. If only we were as impassioned to get our stripes back, still at least we haven't changed from red to blue.

I hate what the owners of Hull and Cardiff are doing to the fabric of their clubs. It's the same story seeing empty seats at an FA Cup semi-final – history is just as important as profit.

Good luck for the rest of the season.

From a Saint who knows where he has been but not necessarily where he is going!

Dear Diary,

Tuesday, 15 April 2014

Today sees the 25th anniversary of the Hillsborough disaster.

Football was very different back in 1989. The replica shirt thing was only just taking off and players' shorts were eye-wateringly short. Cardiff City were in something called the 3rd Division, where the likes of Terry Boyle, Nicky Platnauer and Alan Curtis wore blue shirts sponsored by Buckley's Brewery, the sort of garment which the club sneakily sell today as 'Retro' garments for £25.

On the day of the Hillsborough disaster itself, City lost 1–0 away at Bury, before a crowd of 2,124 – to leave them 17th in the league. City's home game against Southend United, played on Saturday 22 April 1989, kicked off at six minutes past three, in memory of those who had lost their lives in Sheffield – just as our recent game against Southampton did.

Running battles between fans across open terraces were a not uncommon feature of attending football matches in the 1980s, as incidents such as the 1985 Heysel rioting almost brought the game to its knees. We had the Cold War, the Berlin Wall and pop songs about nuclear conflict. Northern Ireland was still at war with itself.

The world looks a lot safer these days, doesn't it? Back then it was hooligans who tried to tear the heart out of the game, though, rather than foreign owners. Not all change is positive, eh?

Dear Diary,

Thursday, 17 April 2014

Well, back to normal today at Car Crash FC. After a couple of days where diary entries have actually been about the football, the Bluebirds have now returned to their quest to win the 'Most Ridiculous Club of the Year' award. A title they have had sewn up for a while actually.

In a 'five-page letter' to the BBC, the club has now claimed that the 3–0 defeat by Crystal Palace should be examined.

The document, sent by club lawyers to the Premier League, alleges Palace boss Tony Pulis knew sporting director Iain Moody was trying to obtain Cardiff's starting line-up before the game. The club claims it has proof that Moody succeeded, and says this breaches League rules. Pulis declined to comment when contacted by the BBC, although Palace previously denied the claims. City reckon clubs should act in good faith to one another and that the whole malarkey calls into serious question the integrity of the match. The Premier League should take 'serious action'.

Oh no ... must we have this all the time????

Dear Diary,

Friday, 18 April 2014

Good Friday

See, I bloody knew it.

This 'Pulis-Gate' thing is now all over the ruddy papers, Sky Sports and the rest.

Here is a text dialogue I had today, for example, with another long-suffering City fan – Richard – who, regrettably, has joined the 'let's-grab-this-straw' brigade:

Rich: 'Check the BBC story now ... f**k me, Jackson, it's been expanded and is incredible. Pulis admitted to Ole after the game he had our line-up. They got moody good 'n' proper on text and e-mail.'

Me: 'It won't make a difference though.'

Rich: 'BBC say City are trying to get the result annulled.'

Me: 'Didn't your missus try that trick once?'

Rich: 'But I read minus 3pts for them mate!! The Blues are staying up!!'

Me: 'Aye ...'

Rich: 'Hey, can you 'n' Andy do a night on the lash 2 May?'

Me: 'Aye ...'

Dear Diary,

Saturday, 19 April 2014

Cardiff City 1 – 1 Stoke City

k/o 3.00 p.m.

There were a few notable City 'firsts' in this game:

One – we picked an unchanged team, for the first time ever under Ole. That was obviously just to confuse Mark Hughes, and the network of spies he was doubtless deploying to discover our team selection. Sparky is never gonna believe Ole would pick the same team!

Two – we finally conceded a penalty. Pity that, because I was hoping we were going to go all the way through the Premier League season without giving one away. Damn!

Another important 'first' in the offing was, can we win two successive Premier League games for the first time this season? The answer to this one was, no. And the reason for this was (as ever) – because we are not good enough for this division.

We had a few half chances in the first half, most of our play going through Dæhli. First he jinked a bit down the left and released Mutch, who fired a shot just wide of Begović's near post. Then Dæhli shot himself, but it was deflected to safety. Then he released Fabio, who was charging forward a lot down that flank – but Fabio slightly over-hit his cross, and it went beyond our attackers.

Of course, the trouble with pressing forward is that you can be susceptible to a counter-attack. And when you have two slow-coaches like Medel and Whittingham in central midfield, you can be very susceptible to a counter-attack. We were reminded of this when Stoke suddenly broke with Stephen Ireland, and had a 2 v. 2 situation. Our (brief) old boy, Peter Odemwingie, was up against Dæhli, and as Ireland played the pass, Odem surged past the young Norseman and fired in a first-time shot which Marshall did well to turn around the post.

To be fair to us, we are generally looking better defensively now, and that looked like it was going to be Stoke's only chance of the half. Then, just before the interval, Odem got the ball in our area but with his back to goal, going nowhere. There was no real goal threat, but regardless of this, Kim decided to clip his ankle, Odem went down – well, what else would you do? – and Howard Webb did not really have much other option than to point to the spot. So our 'clean' penalties conceded record was over.

Of course, it was only a minor irritation, because we knew that Marshall would save the spot kick. Wrong. Arnautović tapped the ball 'up the middle', and it was 1–0 to Stoke.

Could we come back from behind to win? Well, Stoke weren't that good, and we had managed it against Norwich – so maybe. City old boys always score against us (Cameron Jerome at Palace; Aaron Ramsey at home to Arsenal; Joe Ledley at home to Palace) – but maybe Odem had had his chance. Maybe Howard Webb would 'even things up' and give us a penalty, as soon as somebody went down. Of course, we haven't been given a penalty all season, either …

City made a decent start to the second half and, 5 minutes in, won a corner. From the kick, the ball made its way to Kimbo, lurking on the right-hand side of the area. He got to the byline and managed to cut the ball back to Campbell, who got to the ball just ahead of Nzonzi's clumsy challenge. Webb duly pointed to the spot once more.

Whittingham stepped up – but hang on, he's out of practice, he hasn't taken one for a year. We haven't had one for a year. Begović is prancing about, delaying the kick for ages – but to be fair, Whitts keeps his cool and knocks the ball down the middle for 1–1. Tell you what, this kid has got the composure of Beckenbauer!

We have got the bit between our teeth now, and it's like Norwich all over again – we could win it with a second quick goal. Whitts suddenly surges past two players and cuts in from the right – can Whittingham surge? Well, he seemed to – and then crosses for Caulker. Caulker shoots, it hits the keeper, he hits the rebound, it hits the post and comes back out to Cala, who nods it into the net. Mayhem as City take the lead, but why are the Stoke fans celebrating as well? Because they can see the linesman's flag raised, that's why. The 'goal' is disallowed for offside, the momentum goes, and City never really trouble Stoke's goal again.

In the last 10 minutes, Stoke look more likely to win the game than City, and Marshall has to make his usual couple of crucial saves to keep us in it. Stoke sub Jon Walters at one point hits the bar (after Marshall got a fingertip to it), and on another occasion, Marshy blocks Assaidi's shot with his legs, after the other sub had a one-on-one against him.

Zaha had come on for us and had one decent moment, when he surged down the right flank, carrying the ball for 40 yards, and won a corner. Alas, Whittingham came across to take it, and Zaha for some reason thought Whitts was coming to receive a short corner. Result: Whitts is totally surprised and loses possession, Stoke break upfield, and within seconds have won a corner at our end.

This is the problem with having an individualist like Zaha; he often is on nobody else's wavelength. I noticed that when he practised at half-time at Everton, he mainly just kicked the ball on his own, while everyone else was passing to one another. A strange fish indeed.

So can we stay up? No, I don't think so. We needed to win this game, and couldn't. Surely it would have been easier to win against Stoke (not much to play for) at home, than away at Sunderland next week – who have everything to play for. We still can't win two games in a row, and has anybody ever stayed up in the Premier League who didn't manage to win two successive games at some stage in the season? I doubt it.

Our chance of going through the entire season without conceding, or being awarded a penalty, has also gone. But we have still set a Premier League record, as the previous longest run without either of these events happening from the start of the season was twenty-one games. It took us thirty-five games. Whatever else happens to us, we are in the damn record books!

However, Andy has been spouting some rubbish about the Fair Play League. It turns out it is totally different to the disciplinary points table, of which City are near the top. But the Fair Play League takes into account things like 'attractive play' (how do you measure that?), and we are not top of that at all. In fact, we are doing even worse in that than we are in the actual league. If you really want to know, we are bottom. This means we won't be playing Bayern Munich next season, after all.

A funny thing happened after this game: Peter Odemwingie said he was very happy with his reception from the City fans. It was reported in The Times *that we had been chanting his name, as well as the Stoke fans. What actually happened was that the Stokies in the away end kept monotonously doing their 'Peter Odemwingie' chant (which used to be our 'Peter Odemwingie' chant). We got so fed up with it that, after Dæhli beat Odem all ends up, a large contingent of City fans started repeating the chant sarcastically to 'have a pop' back at the Stoke fans. But the sarcasm seems to have totally gone over Odemwingie's head ...*

This leads to the question: how much do the players on the pitch understand of the chants? A few years ago, we had an American striker called Eddie Johnson, who didn't score for about the first twenty times he played for us. But after 50 minutes of every game, everyone at Ninian Park would start chanting 'U-S-A! U-S-A!', urging Dave Jones to bring him on, as if he was Maradona or someone. This was almost totally ironic. Did Eddie Johnson realise it was ironic, or did he think he was being treated 'real good' by the Welsh folk? I have always longed to know ...

Dear Diary,

Sunday, 20 April 2014

Easter Sunday

This bonkers season just keeps on turning up surprises.

Sunderland's unexpected victory over Chelski yesterday, coupled with Liverpool's narrow victory at Carrow Road, seems to have given every team in the bottom three hope.

Oh no, there is that word again ... 'hope'.

City now face Sunderland themselves next Sunday lunch-time, in what could be a relegation decider. Having done Newcastle and back in a day earlier in the year though, Gareth and I are talking ourselves into a luxury overnight trip with the highly efficient TIT tours for £70 return – an outing which even includes a Saturday night out in Middlesbrough.

I will let Tony Jefferies finish his Easter eggs then give him a ring.

Dear Diary,
Tuesday, 22 April 2014

At 10.15 a.m. today, the story broke on Twitter that Ryan Giggs was set to be named as Man United's caretaker manager following David Moyes' sacking. An announcement from the club is expected later today, we understand.

Marvellous. Let's hope Giggsy can remember his Cardiff connections and inspire the Red Devils to stuff Norwich this weekend.

Dear Diary,
Saturday, 26 April 2014

Amazingly, TIT tours elected to set off for tomorrow's game at ... 7.15 a.m. the day before. I was first on the bus as it began its circuitous tour of pre-arranged pick-up points across the city. Tony J. opened the Strongbow. I opened the tuna sandwiches. 'The moon rose ... over an open field ...'

Anyway, we did all that 'laughing on the bus, playing games with the faces' stuff and, having stopped for lunch at, I dunno, Chesterfield, *(The Dusty Miller, Dave ... it was on Sheffield Road in Chesterfield)*, we were safely at Middlesbrough by around 3.00 p.m.

From the hotel window, we gazed across the dull docklands to the Riverside Stadium. 'Boro were home to Barnsley. Hmmmm ... That'd be a new ground for me, No 66.

'What do you reckon, Gareth?'

'I don't mind, Dave, if you want to wander over and see what's happening, we can. I have done the ground but, hey ...'

So we ambled over, under grey northern skies, even this late in April.

Weird sensation this. I have never been outside a football ground while a match was taking place. Empty hot food vans stood amid deserted factories. Discarded cardboard cartons pointed the way to the stadium. From within the Riverside, we could hear the familiar songs and groans of home fans, while the relegation-threatened Tykes told the seagulls overhead how they were 'Barnsley till they die'. The gulls drifted on across the Tees, oblivious to the theatre below. 'Boro legend Wilf

Mannion stood motionless, captured in bronze in an endless, timeless volley of an old leather ball out onto the waves of the enormous grey river. A total of 341 appearances for the one whose blond locks gave him the nickname 'Golden Boy'.

I skulked around a bit hoping to find a half-open door or a gap in the fence somewhere, before Gareth reminded me that football stadiums in 2014 do not have 'gaps in the fence'. These days it's computer-driven turnstiles and burly geezers in hi-vis jackets. Gareth even begged one of these day-glow doormen to let us pop in for five minutes, just so that I could count it as a visit to a new ground. We will leave you to visualise the unmoved response.

So we trudged back across No-man's-land, past Middlehaven, one of the north-east's 'largest and most exciting regeneration projects' according to the information panels ... just as soon as the 'Boat Comes In', no doubt.

A mind-boggling sculpture dominates this deserted, post-industrial landscape, composed of two enormous metal rings, which balance a delicate mesh of steel cables across the grey, windswept docks. Are we invited to contemplate its symbolism of the endless struggle of a steel-hard northern working man, battling against the harsh reality of life in the shipyard? Who knows from so far beneath it? As we wandered on past the Transporter Bridge, a muffled roar pierced the silence. 'Boro had scored again. The Tykes were down. Long trips to Gillingham and Colchester await them. They will tick off MK Dons as a new ground, and moan about their ridiculous Monday night kick-off time for an away game at Sheffield United.

'Barnsley till we die,' they sang. 'Barnsley till we die ...'

Dear Diary,

Sunday, 27 April 2014

Sunderland 4 – 0 Cardiff City

k/o 12.00 noon

This was a bit of a disaster, really. For, although I tried several times, I just could not find my way to the bar.

Sunderland's stadium is impressively big, and boasts, not one, but two statues outside – one of Bob Stokoe, their 1973 FA Cup-winning manager, and the other of a 'typical working-class family going to a game in the 1930s' (even though very few men took their daughters and wives to games in those days).

Yet, despite all these undoubtedly fine accoutrements, it is more or less impossible to find your way to the bar.

To get to the away end, which is 'up in the gods' behind the goal, we had to navigate several flights of stairs, to be met at the top of each flight by an official graffito of witticism adorned on the wall (none of which are very amusing). Then, when we got to the top, we discovered that there is only a food bar on this level – and so you have to go back down to find the bar. Why do they think food is more important than alcohol? In any case, most grounds seem to manage well enough having the food and the drinks counter on the same floor.

Never mind. I was assured by a steward that there was a bar, 'two floors down', so I went to investigate. I trotted two floors down and found only a set of double doors, which appeared to be barred. Continuing downwards, I eventually found myself back by the turnstiles. There, another steward verified the fact that there was a bar, 'three levels up and through the double doors'.

(Where has he gone for this ruddy ale ... Newcastle??)

Okay, so clearly I should have gone through those damn double doors. This time around, I do go through them, although it takes an almighty shove to open the bloody things. But it works – I find myself in a cosy-looking lounge, and think 'Hmm, this is a bit plush', as I make my way eagerly towards the bar.

Before I reach it, I am intercepted by an irate-looking female steward in an officious fluorescent yellow jacket, who informs me crossly that this is a 'members' bar', and 'is totally out of bounds' to the likes of me. I try to explain my plight, and to ascertain where, exactly, the real 'away' bar is, but it soon becomes clear – once she begins actually shoving me – that no useful information is going to be forthcoming from this quarter. So I give up on the much-needed dose of alcohol, and tramp back upstairs to face the horror of the game, stone cold sober.

Okay, so what's the situation here? City need to finish above three teams to stay up: probably Fulham, Sunderland and Norwich. Sunderland have games in hand. The only way we are realistically going to stay above them is if we at least stop them from beating us today. (It might still not be enough.) If we lose this one, we have more or less had it.

The up side is that Sunderland have a woeful home record. Their recent revival has been at Manchester City and Chelsea, two away games. We have been marginally better away than at home recently. So maybe, just maybe, we can get something here.

A fanciful hope indeed. City held their own for 25 minutes, probably enjoying most of the play. Sunderland had not threatened our goal. Everything was going to plan – the idea being to hold them for as long as possible, get them agitated, and then somehow pinch a goal from somewhere (probably another set piece). Like we did at Southampton a couple of weeks back.

The trouble is, you can concede goals from set pieces as well, especially if you don't defend them properly. Just before the half-hour mark, a Larsson corner came in which went over two defenders' heads, and was allowed to bounce (why?). Sunderland danger man, Connor Wickham – three goals in the last two games – ran in ahead of Theo (why was Theo marking him? Why not Caulker or Cala?), and cleverly angled his header back across Marshall, and inside the far post. So, 1–0 Sunderland. Although it was only one goal, it suddenly felt like a massive 'ask' to come back from it.

Just before half-time, Cala dithered over another bouncing ball, eventually attempting to knock it back to Marshall. But he was harried by Wickham, and his pass was far too short. As Wickham ran through onto the ball, Cala resorted to the subtle defensive technique of grabbing hold of his arm and keeping hold of it. The referee allowed Wickham to play on, and the striker rounded Marshall and shot. Cala had managed to get back to the goal line, and cleared the ball. But the sequel to this was that Cala was sent off, and the penalty awarded. No penalties conceded in thirty-four games, and now two in successive games! Borini knocked it in, and we were 2–0 down.

The second half was quite painful to watch, as Ole made substitutions to try to rescue the game. Are we really going to win from 2 goals and a man down? We can't normally win games starting 'level pegging' with eleven men!

The almost inevitable result was that we looked more and more hapless, and conceded 2 further goals. Borini threaded a through ball for sub Giaccherini to run onto, and he knocked it past Marshall at his near post. Then Wickham out-jumped Theo from another corner. (Again: why is Theo marking him?!)

4-0 looks bad, and this game certainly felt bad. If you lose games like this 4-0 at this stage of the season, there is only one way you are going, and that is down. We are now bottom of the table, and it would be difficult to argue that we didn't deserve to be there.

Everyone in the away end now seems to have accepted our fate. 'F**k Man. Utd, it's Brentford away!' Actually, that doesn't sound too bad. At least in the Championship, we might be able to win a few games.

And I might just be able to get a drink.

Dear Diary,

Monday, 28 April 2014

Gary Neville and Jamie Carragher spent most of today debating the question of who deserves to be named in the Premier League team of 2013/14 on Sky Sports.

The two pundits agreed on eight of the players to feature in the dream team (Gerrard, Terry, Suarez etc.) but relied on a Twitter vote to decide who should play in goal, at left back and on the right-hand side of midfield after failing to agree on these positions.

David Marshall polled an amazing (though fully deserved) 83 per cent in this poll, seeing off Chelsea's Petr Cech, who polled only 17 per cent. Carragher (who had gone for Marshall in the first place) told Sky how our 'Super Scottish Stopper' Marsh had made four or five saves this season that he had thought 'Top save, I expected that to go in.' He was the only keeper Carra could think of who had made those types of saves.

But then we knew that already, didn't we?

Dear Diary,

Tuesday, 29 April 2014

Cardiff City Football Club today confirmed that Juan Cala has been charged with improper conduct by the FA following an alleged incident in or around the tunnel area after the Sunderland game. He has until 6.00 p.m. on Thursday 1 May to respond to the charge.

And that's all we know. No clues at all as to what sort of mischief the red-carded Spaniard got up to. Message boards were awash with speculative stories, none of which made it past the publisher's lawyers I am afraid.

Two games to go ...

Ten

NUTS
IN MAY

Dear Diary,

Friday, 2 May 2014

And so we face, the final curtain ...

A long, tortuous year has seen the dark nights of winter replaced by the blossom of May. The world has seen the loss of Bob Hoskins, Sue Townsend and my cat, Medi. And the media spotlight has focused on Cardiff City like never before.

If we weren't sure how big this Premier League thing was before the season began, we bloody well know it now. The club has gone from the ecstasy of triumph over Man. City, to debacles against sides who finished below us last season. We have been on the front pages more than the back, so it seems. Yet with just two games left, the wounded patient somehow still clings to life. Do we all have the emotional energy for one last throw of the dice? People I know have already set off on yet another long journey to the north-east, as the juxtaposition of fixtures this week means that, incredibly, victory over Newcastle United – a club in turmoil with little to play for – could see us out of the bottom three at 5.00 p.m. tomorrow with just one home game left to negotiate.

And it'd be just like us to bloody go and do that, wouldn't it?

Dear Diary,

Saturday, 3 May 2014

Newcastle United 3 – 0 Cardiff City

k/o 3.00 p.m.

This was a tight game, which ended in another collapse. We are having too many of these 3-0 and 4-0 defeats. It makes us look like a poor team ...

There were five changes for this game, but Ole cannot be blamed this time, as a lot of the squad were ill. It became obvious why when newly restored Gunnarsson strode onto the pitch sporting a horrendous beard, a truly gruesome growth the likes of which we have not seen since the days of Trevor Hockey (ask your father!). Perhaps Gunnar has grown it since the 'leaked team sheet affair', hoping that Ole will forget who he is, and pick him again.

More to the point, could City stop the 'leaking goals affair' which has been going on for the past few weeks? Well, we made a decent start. We survived an early scare, then nearly took the lead when Fabio put in a decent high cross. Mutch had got forward and challenged the Geordies' keeper, Tim Krul, who could only punch the ball away. It fell to Fraizer Campbell, admittedly at an awkward height – and Campbell's acrobatic half-volley drifted harmlessly wide of an open goal. With more composure, Campbell might have taken a touch first, and then shot.

We were punished for this miss after 18 minutes, when Sissoko beat Declan John down our left, and crossed to the far post. Caulker had forgotten to mark Shola Ameobi. As he 'ball watched', it sailed over him, and Ameobi nodded it into the empty net: 1-0 Newcy.

This stirred the home side, and we nearly went 2 down when Sissoko hit a shot which deflected onto our post, and bounced to safety.

Having survived this, we nearly scored when Zaha suddenly came to life. The often invisible wing man, now operating on the left, pushed the ball outside one defender, cut inside another, and then tried to sneak the ball inside Krul's near post.

Krul was wrong-footed, but managed to stop the ball with his toe cap. Cruel!

Zaha had another chance when he broke into space with only the keeper to beat. But before he could shoot, Debuchy managed to slide in and get the ball away from him. And that five-minute spurt of action was about all we saw from the enigmatic Wilfried.

On 69 minutes, there was a curious semi-walkout from some of the home fans, in protest at their club not winning any trophies since 1969. We have done the same kind of thing on the 27-minute mark, of course. When do Rochdale fans stage their walkouts?

With 20 minutes to go, we were still in it. Maybe we could come back and at least draw. Maybe other results would go our way. Maybe we would at least take the relegation battle right down to the final game of the season.

Suddenly, we were having a go. Fabio put another cross in, Gunnar cushioned a header for Kenwyne, a sub, who shot from close range – blocked by Krul. Then another cross came in, Krul fumbled it, the ball fell to Gunnar. He shot and seemed certain to score, but Geordie skipper Coloccini, frantically covering, managed to hack it off the line. I think we all knew 'the game was up' when that one didn't go in.

Then came the collapse. After all the City pressure, Newcastle had one chance – and scored. Mind you, we had three defenders back, and they only had one man in our area (Remy). But as usual in Ole's curious system of 'defending', nobody went to mark Remy (Caulker being the main culprit once more), the ball (inevitably) came to him, and he tucked it in the net.

A couple of minutes later, Steven Taylor scored the 3rd from a corner, and we had another embarrassing-looking defeat on our hands.

News came through that Sunderland had won at Old Trafford. Cardiff City were officially relegated.

Dear Diary,
Sunday, 4 May 2014

Here's what I sang on the pub karaoke night last night:

Well, I never felt more like crying all night
'Cause everything's wrong
And nothing is right, without you
You got me singing the blues

The moon and stars no longer shine
The dream is gone I thought was mine.
There's nothing left for me to do
But cry-y-y over you

Somehow it just seemed like the right thing to do at the time.

Dear Diary,
Monday, 5 May 2014

Well, with the body not yet cold in the grave, the post mortems have already commenced.

Rob Phillips began the autopsy as soon as the final whistle sounded on Saturday, offering Radio Wales listeners a damning indictment of the club's catastrophic attempts to make a fist of things this season. Yesterday's *Wales on Sunday* described the campaign as 'truly awful' while today's *Western Mail* (a journal yet to feature in these pages, I think) continued the theme, reporting how City were 'out of their depth'. Everyone is making the right noises about next season, but already there is talk of relegation clauses included in the contracts of some of Malky's big money signings. It could be a long, lonely summer.

And still, still, the fans cry out for a return to blue.

Dear Diary,
Wednesday, 7 May 2014

Hey Gareth, let's cheer ourselves up a bit, shall we? It's the Supporters' Club Player of the Year Do tonight. Do you fancy it?

What, on a Wednesday night? In some dusty venue like the Llandaff Institute?

No, no. Straight up. It's a posh do this year. I got chance of tickets. They present the end of season awards too, all the players will be there. We might even meet Don Cowie.

You are not selling it to me, Dave. How much are the tickets?
£45.

Forty Five Quid!!!!??? FFS Dave! Let's do our own awards and save a fortune.

And so we did ...

Player of the Year	Marshall
	Oh come on, Dave ... is that the best we can do. It's Marshall by a mile.
Okay, okay ...	*Ah, that's better. Bit of thought needed there.*
Best Outfield Player	*To be honest though, we have been so poor that it's hard to see any other consistent player. Maybe if Noone had been fitter? And Jordan Mutch shone in flashes I guess, with some good goals to boot.*
	I am going for Campbell.
	He is crap, Dave!
	He is a trier ... never stopped running.
	Jeez ...
Best Performance	*Man. City at home.*
	Jacks at home.
Worst Performance	*Cardiff 0 Hull 4*
	Palace.
	Home or Away?
	Both.
Best Goal	*Hmmm. Campbell's against Man. U. A great team goal.*
	I am going for Dæhli's dramatic late equaliser against West Brom. Football is all about the passion, the moment, and the hope. That goal had all three.
Fave Away Ground	*I'd say Everton. Good atmosphere, proper old school stadium and a decent view down the side of the pitch next to the Evertonians.*
	For me it was the Etihad.
	It reeks of Premier League.

Biggest Disappointment	*Malky's signings who failed to deliver. They ranged from moderate to atrocious.* All the bloody off-the-field nonsense.
Most Disappointing Player	*Has to be Cornelius. Zaha was a let-down too but he didn't cost £8 million.* Yeah, I wanted so much to love Zaha, but he gave me nothing. *Like that bird in Sheffield?* Hey, take it easy mate ...
Young Player of the Year	*Declan John.* I agree. 'Highly Commended' certificate to Dæhli for his bedroom wall too perhaps.
Non City Player of the Year	*I am not sure what you mean, Dave ...* Yaya Touré. *Oh I see. Let me come back to you on that one. Ramsey perhaps, before he was injured.*
And finally, our hopes for next season?	*Just some kind of ruddy stability at the club. The finances, the team selection ... can we just have some order to the chaos?* You just want Cardiff City to be a proper football club again? *Exactly. Go on then , it's your go ...* Me? Well, apart from the obvious (see tatty scarf on front cover), I think I just want the focus to be on the football again, and not the catalogue of embarrassments that have marred a historic season. *Good luck with getting that engraved on an award, Dave ...*

Dear Diary,

Thursday, 8 May 2014

Last night's victory for Sunderland over West Brom. virtually condemns Norwich City to the championship. A crumb of comfort for me is that this means that next season, I will have visited every ground in the Premier League.

Yeah, but you are counting that trip to the Emirates for a Youth Cup tie in that, aren't you?

Too right I am. Aaron Ramsay played for us that night – Cup match that was. I think they had over 13,000 there.

Blimey, I have been to first team games with much less than that.

Exactly.

Dear Diary,
Friday, 9 May 2014

Right, that's it. I have officially 'had a gutsful' of this season. A right ruddy gutsful.

Driving peacefully home along the M4 this evening, my slumber was disturbed by yet another bewildering development from the Cardiff City Stadium. Just as the season was whimpering to a close, there is one last nail to hammer into our souls.

For today, we learn that Malky has reached a 'settlement agreement' dropping all claims against the club. Nothing wrong with that of course, but in a carefully worded statement, the big Scotsman talks of the sheer joy he experienced at Cardiff City, his gratitude to Tan for making it all happen and a forelock-tugging acknowledgement that 'without him (i.e. Tan) this would not have been possible'. He even goes on to apologise to Tan 'without reservation'.

I mean, really??? Does all this sound right to you?

And then the news goes viral. CCFC is once more all over the media ... with the sensational news that Malky (and Moody) have 'apologised' while the carefully worded statements are nailed to the palace gates. Tim Hartley called the language 'conciliatory' though admitted we may never know the truth. Pat Nevin said, 'it doesn't stack up'.

Me, I have had a gutsful.

A right, ruddy gutsful.

Dear Diary,
Saturday, 10 May 2014

BBC reporter Rob Phillips 'hotfooted it' (to use his words) to London today for another remarkable interview with Mr Tan.

Tan's revelations included expressing his disappointment that the away fans at the game in Newcastle all wore blue, while the team had turned out in red. He also slightly reneged on his promise to turn his debt into equity, and indicated his interest in offering the fans a seat on the board. I may revisit my decision not to stand for the Trust Board if that is true.

Rob Phillips, to his credit, picked up the mantle and confronted Tan directly on the question of the kit colour. Tan – who cannot fail to have noticed the growing strength of feeling over this issue – responded with a carefully worded mumble about how he might be prepared to look at things again and consider a 'compromise' if the club returned to the Premier League.

I am not jumping up and down over this, though. This was a promise based on something that hasn't even happened yet and, indeed, may not happen at all. That's like me promising my Dad (Happy Birthday, Dad, by the way …) a new Ferrari if I win the lottery.

But it means that the noises we are making over the club colours are at least hitting home. Time to be even noisier, I reckon!

Dear Diary,

Sunday, 11 May 2014

Cardiff City 1 – 2 Chelsea

k/o 3.00 p.m.

The final League game of the season – and, for all I know, our last ever Premier League fixture – took place on a sunny Sunday afternoon in front of a sea of blue shirts.

Supporters' groups had called for a show of solidarity from all City fans over the 'blue versus red' issue. There was a strong response, and there were very few red shirts visible (although owner Vincent Tan turned up in one). Even the 'happy families, mums, dads and kids' brigades had the sense to wear something blue, just this once, instead of the usual red.

And so, when the 'blue' chants began, scarves were raised in what seemed an absolutely pure blue stadium. Even the away end was wearing blue!

This battle over colours has been going on for two years now. I don't think I've mentioned it before in this book. It's a hot potato alright, but every man and his dog has had his say on the matter, so I haven't bothered. All I can say now is, if you've got a stadium full of blue shirts and blue scarves, supporting a home team playing in red – well, it's the ultimate absurdity, really. If Tan thinks he is just 'being a businessman', then he needs to go back to business school. Rule one: don't alienate your own customers!

As well as all the blue scarves, we also had a load of balloons on the pitch, celebrating – what, exactly? Our season in the Premier League? Wasn't much to celebrate really, was there? Maybe they weren't 'Cardiff City' balloons, but were rather 'Premier League' ones, put there so that we could celebrate the basic concept of the Premier League.

Anyway, whoever's balloons they were, they came in handy after a quarter of an hour, when Torres broke away from our defenders and rounded Marshall, only to be 'tackled' by one of the balloons. By the time Torres had sidestepped the inflatable, Caulker had got back to clear the Spaniard's shot off the line.

City then took an unlikely lead from their first attack of the game. Bellamy, receiving the ball near halfway with his back to goal, turned and ran with the ball. When he got within shooting range, he let fly with a left-footed blast which sharply deflected off the Chelsea right-back, Azpele – no, Azpile – no, Az – which deflected off the Basque lad at right-back. The deflection completely wrong-footed Schwarzer, and City were in front. Just like we were at Stamford Bridge!

The goal was a bit of a fluke, but in Bellers' defence, at least he did shoot. Too many times this season, when City have got into those kinds of position, everyone's been allergic to having a go.

We looked good at other times, too. Fabio and Dæhli looked to be striking up an understanding on the right, and frequently one of them would surge into space. Dæhli is a strange-looking character – he is so low-slung, he waddles rather than runs, but once he gets moving, he can actually 'motor' past defenders. He could emerge as a star in the Championship next season – if he is still here ...

At one point a flowing move ended with Mutch knocking the ball forward for Campbell to run onto – only Campbell, as usual, had made a different run, and was going the wrong way – and so the move petered out. But at least City were showing something.

Half-time arrived, and Chelsea still hadn't scored. Could an unforeseen win be on the cards? Not that it would have mattered. This game was a bit of a non-event, for them as well as us. When this fixture was published, we all thought, hmm, probably this will be a crucial affair, Chelsea going for the title, and us needing a point to stay up – something like that. But we were relegated a game beforehand, and Chelsea had already blown the title. So, after a season of anticipation, there turned out to be absolutely bugger all on the damn game.

A lot of the time, Chelsea seemed to play as if it didn't really matter. Mourinho stood on the touchline, but with a face like a slapped arse. He didn't really want to be here, at a meaningless match, when the title was being decided somewhere else. For once, he could not be the centre of attention – and you could see it was killing him.

Anyway, just when I thought maybe Chelsea weren't even interested enough in the game to win it, they came back and won it. Schürrle, a sub, equalised on 72 minutes, and 3 minutes later, Torres got the winner. I can't remember how these goals were scored, and – to be honest – I am no longer interested enough in this damn Premier League to check the match reports and YouTube clips.

The season is now over. Thank God for that. Next season we are back in the Championship. We will not be as bad in the Championship as we were in the Premier League.

I think the Championship is a very nice league to be in.

EPILOGUE

Epilogue ... with Jason Perry.

Well, that was our take on the season. But what do we know? We are just two blokes in the pub, after all. So we added a third, and a proper expert he was too, as we turned to our resident pundit and City legend, Jason Perry.

Yeah, a proper psychoanalysis session!

So Jason, what did you think of the season as a whole?

My high points were seeing the Cardiff City players running out at Upton Park for the first time in the Premier League; beating the eventual Premier League champions Man. City at home; and of course, beating our fiercest rivals.

The derby win allowed me to discuss in great detail with anybody with a Swansea background, a minute by minute breakdown of Cardiff's victory in the Premiership's first ever Welsh derby. Can't be taken away!

Yeah, I guess there were some early highs, but it soon faded, didn't it?

Undoubtedly the turning point of the season was the sacking of Malky Mackay midway through the season. Whilst we can argue about style of play, transfers and ifs and buts ... the side were out of the bottom three and had direction, organisation and a game plan. Would it have kept us up? We can only guess this, but you have more chance if you have belief, organisation and are working collectively as a team.

But the stats show that we were actually getting worse under Malky.

How do you work that out, Gareth?

We won four games under him – but three of them were in the first ten games. We only managed a single win in his last eight, something the media never mention. After the first ten games, we averaged 1.2 points per game. In the next eight, it slumped to 0.625, which was worse than Ole's success rate.

That's hard to believe, isn't it? What did you think of the OGS appointment then, Jason? Were the club right to sack Malky?

When asked the question at the time about Malky's departure, I stated my concerns that the board had no experience, knowledge or criteria on which to pick the next manager. It's easy to sack a manager, but very difficult to make the correct appointment that would make the change a smooth transition and increase the club's chances of survival. Cardiff went for a completely opposite style of play, and with little time to change personnel or implement such a drastic change in strategy. I'm sure the present manager is looking forward to a preseason and time on the training ground with the players who he believes can turn instruction into performances.

Player for player, there was little difference between City under Malky or Ole. Both had Marshy in goal; Ole perhaps preferred Fabio to French Kev at right-back and MM went for Taylor over Declan at left-back.

The full-back spot was a problem all season. Fabio offers little defensively and, much as I like Declan, he is still learning the ropes.

In central defence, Malky had Caulker and Turner. Lots of Bluebirds complained that Turner couldn't pass. Ole eventually went for Caulker and Cala, but Cal couldn't challenge for the ball in my opinion. In midfield MM kept picking Medel and Whittingham – week in, week out. Out wide Ole didn't pick Craig Noone for certain games – and he only started three times under Malky.

Noone was MOTM at Man. City.

Malky generally favoured a 4-5-1 system with Campbell as the lone striker, but so did OGS eventually, so nothing much actually changed.

What did you think of Campbell up top, Jason? Gareth and I have different views!

For me, Frazier Campbell can hold his head up high with his season representing the Bluebirds. He comes across as an honest, brave and hard-working centre forward who understands his full role in a team. Not one minute did I see him sulk or shy away from his defensive responsibilities when, at times, he was starved of service. He continued to make intelligent runs, playing off the defenders' shoulder and stretching them at every opportunity.

However, people may argue that strikers are judged by the amount of goals they score and, at times, he did not look a natural goal scorer in front of goal, I agree, but I'm sure that with the attitude and determination he has shown for Cardiff he will improve in this department. He has proven he is a Premier League player, and City will do well to keep him for the 2014/15 Championship season. A great buy for us at such a bargain price. I hope no other team is saying the same thing about him next season.

We mentioned the highs. What were the low points?

Relegation, and seeing the side run out in red still doesn't feel right. The Bluebirds' lethargic performance and defeat in the away tie at the Liberty. Still you never do remember the second time of anything, only the first!! The biggest disappointments were our performances and results against the sides around the bottom of the table – Hull City, Crystal Palace and Sunderland etc. Every fan would have said at the start of the season ... 'you have to beat the teams around you!'

Tell us, Jason, you have been in the dressing room, does the off-the-field stuff affect the players at all?

It shouldn't, but it depends on the squad's character and the individual player circumstances, including his contract, relationship with the previous manager or board etc. With thought, you can even use such boardroom unrest to bring the squad closer together, increase focus, togetherness and belief. Creating that something that the whole squad feels strong enough to fight for, or against, is the most powerful tool of motivation. It creates a powerful feeling within us, an 'us-against-them' or siege culture within the changing room. This takes great planning and has to be continually managed throughout the season.

Chelsea manager Jose Mourinho is the master of this!!!! He creates a belief or fight that brings the whole club together, including players, staff, employees and fans. They will do anything to fight against that something, or for that something.

The Cardiff City fans provided their own example of this, fighting for a return to blue and the club's identity. A strong belief brings people together, something to fight for and to make the sacrifices to succeed. If things were settled in the boardroom, with planning, thought and support from the owners, we could have created that strong and positive belief of 'us-against-them' throughout the WHOLE club, which would have worked for all of us and helped our club stay in the Premier League. This has to be driven from the manager and supported by the board. Instead, decisions from the top created a difference of opinion and divide within the club.

Wales' capital city playing in the Premier League for the first time should have been an obvious factor to work with. Do the Premier League really want us? Referee decisions etc., etc. However, the decision-makers within the club must have an understanding of such motivational tools, and not work against one of the biggest energisers and motivational factors a team can have – your own fans!

So what are our hopes for next season, then?

For the board to have constructive dialogue with the fans. A change to blue, and keep red as the away kit, so as not to isolate those who believed that it was more of a question of the club going under if revenue wasn't raised abroad by the change of colour. I myself was made to believe this by board members. And of course promotion to the Premiership!

Good stuff, Jase – any other final thoughts?

If the club adopts this more positive, open and expansive football, then we have to stick with it, wins and losses, and make it the club's long-term identity and strategy. The board need to gain a better understanding of what makes a manager fit our identity, and not change this for each new manager at the club.

The only certainty in football management is getting the sack or managers leaving for a fresh challenge. This means there will always be change at management level, and these transition periods must be smooth and only enhance and build on the previous manager's work. A director of football might be the answer?

Gareth?

A few seasons ago, a mate of mine surprised me when he told me that he had no interest in going up to the Premier League if we were getting beat every week, he would rather stay in the Championship. I thought it would be interesting to see City take on the top sides every week, but the Premier League is the same as any other division. It's no fun if you are struggling all the time, particularly if you can't win your home games.

After a while you don't look at the table or even watch Match of the Day*! Maybe we will have more fun in the Championship, and win more games. But now we have been given a glimpse of the Promised Land, will we have the same motivation going into next season?*

I know what you mean ... things just won't be the same as last year, despite all the craziness!

Dear Diary,

Friday, 11 July 2014

Right, now where is Gareth's number, it's here somewhere ...
Let me see, ah, here we go, 07592 ...

(rings ...)
(... silence)
(rings again ...)
'... ullo??'
'Gareth, Gareth, it's me. You seen the *Echo*?'
'Uhm ...'
'The *Echo*. You seen today's *Echo*?'
'What time is it, Dave?'
'Almost 7.30 a.m.'
'Bloody hell Dave!'
'Anyway, the *Echo*?'
'Do what??'
'More pre-season friendlies have been announced. We play Bath City away tomorrow. Shall we go? Shall we??'
'Dave, I'm still in ruddy bed ...'
'Ah come on, it'll be a laugh. It's only up the road. I can drive and we can even crash at a B&B and make a night of it. I can't wait to see the new signings in action. Guerra scored 72 goals in 149 appearances for Real Valladolid!'
(pauses ...)
(pauses ...)
'Yeah!!!! Why not. Let's go!'
'Yay!!!'
'Bluebirds!!!!!!!!'

Lightning Source UK Ltd.
Milton Keynes UK
UKOW04f0019270814

237598UK00001B/2/P